# AGED IN CHANGING SOCIAL SYSTEM

## *THEIR PROBLEMS*

# AGED IN CHANGING SOCIAL SYSTEM
## *THEIR PROBLEMS*

*By*

**N.K. Behura**

*&*

**R.P. Mohanty**

*Nabakrushna Choudhury Centre for Development Studies, Orissa Bhubaneswar–751 013*

**DISCOVERY PUBLISHING HOUSE**
**NEW DELHI-110002**

First Published-2005
Reprinted-2014

ISBN 978 81 7141 923 4



*Published by*

**DISCOVERY PUBLISHING HOUSE**
4831/24, Ansari Road, Prahlad Street,
Darya Ganj, New Delhi-110002 (India)
Phone: 23279245 • Fax: 91-11-23253475
E-mail:dphtemp@indiatimes.com

*Printed at:*

Shree Balaji Art Press

# Foreword

India is a vast country with diverse ethnic groups, languages and cultures. At the macro-level these diversities may not be conspicuous, but at the macro-level these are palpable. Indian population is heterogeneous, and therefore, macro-level information as available in the census reports, are not helpful for generalisation. One finds at the ground level ethno-cultural variations. Occupation, caste composition, economy, practice of religion and educational status all vary in some way or the other. There are of course a lot of similarities among the people. Hence, in the fast changing Indian society, there is an urgent need for understanding the current socio-cultural situations through micro-studies. The present project, sponsored by the Nabakrushna Choudhury Centre for Development Studies, Orissa, is a step in that direction. There have not been adequate studies in Orissa on socio-economic condition of the aged, where 48 per cent of the population is below the poverty line. The present study on the aged has been carried out in some fringe villages of Bhubaneswar city.

The aged have manifold problems both in rural and urban societies. In several instances they are treated as unwanted persons and parasites. A persons after losing his/her vim, vigour and vitality in the old-age becomes utterly helpless and is forced to depend on others. Society has responsibilities towards the aged, and although they are in the decline, they constitute the senior generation in the society and are treated as the sources of wisdom.

Aging is a biological process and socio-cultural concept too. Hence, position and treatment of the aged vary from culture to culture.

The number of aged persons is on the increase decades world over due to the availability of better health care facilities in developed as well as in developing countries. In developing countries access to modern health care facilities is meager and scanty because of poor economic condition and lack of awareness about desirable healthy life. Nevertheless, Central and State governments have been trying to provide basic medical facilities to all. Improvement in living conditions and rise of the general quality of life and effective measures for birth control could be attributed to this emerging phenomenon, particularly in the developing countries. Aged population in the developing countries is going to outnumber such population in the developed countries.

In the decades to come, there is a possibility of greater concentration of the aged in the rural areas of developing countries. The problem of the aged in urban areas may be less acute because people in rural areas are less informed, continue to depend on agriculture, and vocational occupations. In contrasts to this, most people in urban areas have income from various non-agricultural sources.

Social security in India is in a nascent stage. Old-age homes are sporadic and the concept of old-age home is still not within the range of knowledge of rural masses. However, the old people living in the rural areas of developing countries will be in misery primarily for two reasons, namely (i) economically they are not unproductive and (ii) their consequential social alienation. The problem may assume gigantic proposition for lack of resources to initiate effective measures. India as a part of the developing countries is no exception. Assessment of the magnitude of the problem is a prime importance. Socio-economic characteristics are to be ascertained for evolving appropriate strategies and programmes for redressal of their suffering. Rapid population growth, lack of education and modern public health care services, denudation of life-supporting resources, urbanisation and liberalisation have all contributed to the weakening of traditional corporate cultural values. Thus, individualism is on the rise. As a result, in several cases, neglect and suffering of the aged is a matter of concern. It is expressed that the civil society must develop strategies so as to ameliorate the plight and tribulations of the aged.

With the growing number of aged in our country in the background of fast paces of changes all around and disintegration of joint family system, it is highly essential to plan appropriate strategy for providing shelter and minimum facilities for the aged to lead a desirably graceful life.

The present piece of research is in the form of a pilot study. It will provide comprehensive information about the aged in Oriya society, that is, the socio-economic background of the aged, their special problems concerning, to the mode of living, their relationship with their family members, kins, neighbours and their socio-economic support system, food and narcotic habits, health, diseases and treatment process, leisure and recreational activities, withdrawal of pension etc.

In most cases the old person are viewed as socio-economic burdens rather than assets. It is because, the old people do not directly participate in active productive activities excepting those who continue to draw monthly income, which is grabbed, by their adults sons and daughters-in-law.

The study is primarily based on those who are retired from government and other organised sectors after attaining to the age of superannuation. But many of them are still mentally and physically active and capable. They can render several services to the society through their rich experience and knowledge. But there is no scope for them in the state of Orissa. It should be explored as to how their mature services can be used in the interest of the society. They can make substantial contribution to the process of socio-economic development.

I am happy to note that the study throws a great deal of insight into the problems of the aged in Oriya Middle Class Caste Hindu families in some selected fringe villages of Bhubaneswar city. Due to some improvement in medical facilities and increased awareness among the people to take preventive measures, there is gradual improvement in longevity of the people even in rural areas, and particularly in the neighbourhood of urban centres. And further, due to disintegration of the joint family system, in many places, the aged people are leading lonely life which cause a number of tensions with consequent distress and agony. This problem has assumed tremendous importance in the present day economic and social set-up.

I congratulate Prof. N.K. Behura, Honorary Fellow of the NKC Centre and Dr. Ramesh Prasad Mohanty of the centre for their penetrating analysis in making such an important study which has great relevance for the research workers of the Centre to pursue other related matters which may be of much use to take adequate measures to improve the quality of life of aged people. Both of them deserve our commendation for their strenuous work in completing such a worthwhile study within such a short period of time. We are grateful to Prof. N.K. Behura for his genuine endeavour to improve the research activities of the Centre. He is, as a matter of fact, a great asset and we hope that his continued association will improve the image of the Centre.

I hope that this book will be very useful for academicians, researchers, students, NGO activists, administrators and all those who are interested in gerontological studies.

**(Prof. B. Misra)**

Former Director and Chairman
and at present Research Advisor,
N.K.C. Centre for Development Studies,
Orissa

# Preface

Since last few decades social gerontology has been an important discipline of study in anthropology because the role and the social status of the elderly persons are abating at an alarming rate in both the patriarchal and matriarchal societies. This problem has emerged as an outgrowth of population explosion in many populous countries of the world as over-population is always lethalic to institutionalised life at familial level or to the social systems as a whole. In such countries, particularly in India, the traditional social systems have been disintegrated and the filial generations have become very self-centred, egocentric and individualistic in nature because of the competition for leading a comfortable life in over-denuded socio-ecological niches where the imbalance between the existing population and the available resources for utilisation is very acute. This has certainly diminished the social values or cultural practices of honouring or giving the due social status to the aged in our societies. As a result, it is apprehended that their problems would accrue in future and hence be interminable unless the social systems are mended. This would in other way protect the inherent culture specific social values and the equation of interpersonal dependency among members at the familial level or at the level of the society as a whole.

With these social perspectives, we have attempted to point out the social problems of some particular sections of the aged, viz, the pensioners and their spouses and non-pensioners who belong to Oriya middle class caste Hindu families and reside on the outskirts of Bhubaneswar city, the state capital of Orissa.

Since the filial generations and consistently forgetting their role perspectives towards the well-being of their old parents and getting away from their moral duties because of their deeper insight for leading an independent life style, in this report we have meticulously pinpointed some important situational aspects like living arrangement of the aged, their economic support, work participation and contribution of physical labour towards the family—economy. Some other aspects of the problem like generation gap between the aged and other family members, social relationship of the aged with the members of ascending and descending generations and their involvement in the process of decision-making at the household and community levels during any crisis or difficult situations have been dealt with. Apart from all these aspects, a vivid picture on their food habits, status of health and the process of treatment of the diseases have also been discussed.

The aged are traditionally considered as the source of wisdom and hence are available assets. But certainly, even though the aged are helpful to the family and society in myriad ways, they are neglected on various spheres of the daily life. Most of them are fed up with the failed promises of familial life and suffer from psychological trauma and mental distress and in many cases their distress condition and painful annoyance remain obscure for the public. Thus, the need of studying the problems of the aged has become an urgent concern for all of us with a view to safeguarding their rights and interests and thereby help in bringing out a healthy and problem free society.

We are fortunate enough to have been privileged to undertake such a crucial study which is highly essential at the present time. But we could not study some of the stirring aspects of the problems thoroughly as the project was time bound and based on internal funding and hence was lacking sufficient manpower to do the job.

We express our deep gratitude to Professor B. Misra, Chairman, Nabakrushna Choudhury Centre for Development Studies, for having entrusted to us the research project. At the same time we are also grateful to Professor G.C. Kar, Director, Nabakrushna Choudhury Centre for Development Studies, for encouraging us and rendering all the necessary assistance as and when required during the entire period of study.

We extend our sincere thanks to the informants for their co-operation which they extended to us during the survey period. We record our thankfulness for all of them.

We hope that this book will be very useful to the researchers, academicians, administrators, social planners and the NGO activists who are concerned with the problems of the aged and are actively working for the well-being of these people.

N.K. Behura

R.P. Mohanty

# Contents

# Glossary

| | | |
|---|---|---|
| *Arthashāstra* | : | Ancient law book on management of state finance, written by Kautilya |
| *Āshram* | : | A place of religious retreat for Hindus |
| *Astaprahari* | : | Ritual performed for twenty-four hours collectively in devotional praise of lord Krishna. Devotees sing continuously for twenty-four hours in turn without any break |
| *Bhāgavat Gita* | : | An important religious text of Hindus. In this text Lord Krishna explains the ethics of war to Arjun; an epic hero |
| *Bhāgavatghar* | : | Village sacred cottage where Lord Krishna is generally worshipped |
| *Bidi* | : | An indigenous smoke, i.e., tobacco rolled in kendu (Diospyrosm tovoxylon) leaf |
| *Brāhmin* | : | Priest or a member of the highest varna who mediates between devotees and the gods and deities |
| *Chasā* | : | Farming caste |
| *Dayā* | : | Sense of kindness |
| *Dayābhag* | : | A traditional system of land ownership by which a man is the sole authority of the landed properties he has. His progenies cannot claim a share of it so long as the head of the household is alive. They can have their share at the sweet will of their father. It is generally prevalent in Bengal, Assam and Tripura. |
| *Devi* | : | Goddess |
| *Dharma* | : | Religion |

| | | |
|---|---|---|
| *Gauda* | : | Cattle herder or milkman who traditionally breeds cattle and subsists on sale of milk or milk products |
| *Jyotish* | : | Village astrologer |
| *Kamāra* | : | Blacksmith |
| *Karan* | : | A member of the scribe caste |
| *Khaini* | : | Indigenous tobacco powder |
| *Khandāyat* | : | A member of militia caste |
| *Laxmi* | : | Presiding goddess of wealth of fortune |
| *Mahābhārat* | : | An important religious text of Hindus. It explain how the great *Mahabharat* war occurred |
| *Mahimādharma* | : | A religious sect opposed to caste system. It advocates equality of all human begins without caste discrimination |
| *Mitākshyar* | : | A system by which ancient or paternal landed properties are automatically transcended to the children after the death of their father in the male's line. It is prevalent in all Indian states excepting Bengal, Assam and Tripura |
| *Pasā* | : | An indigenous ancient Indian game; played on a format in 2 x 2 basis which has a place in *Mahabharat* epic |
| *Patta* | : | Document relating to record of right on landed properties |
| *Ramāyan* | : | An important religious text of Hindus in which Lord Rama is the hero or an ideal person |
| *Srādha* | : | Ancestral worship that is done annually by the eldest son of the deceased person |
| *Sundhi* | : | A caste traditionally trading in alcohol |
| *Teli* | : | A member of traditionally oil-crushing caste |
| *Tamākhu* | : | Tobacco paste prepared with lime |
| *Thākurghar* | : | Temple of village deity |
| *Trinathmelā* | : | Worshipping of three important Hindu deities, viz, *Brahma Vishnu* and *Maheswar* by the Hindus |

# 1

# Introduction

## Introduction

Becoming old is a biological process and it occurs naturally to all living organisms. Man is not an exception to it. When a human baby is born, it grows, attains its childhood, adulthood and finally becomes old and ultimately passes away. This is inevitable, but although the process of aging is a biological phenomenon it is very much conditional to or associated with various social factors, cultural values, norms and regulations to a great extent. So, during the course of lifetime of a human being, he/she takes up various role-performances to play depending upon its age and prevailing societal norms and cultural heritage. In this context Neugarten and others say that, "In all societies age is one of the bases for the ascription of status and one of the underlying dimensions by which social interaction is regulated" (1980-161). Hence, within this culture-based social framework, conscious parents nourish their children with utmost care, educate them with highest sincerity and socialise them as to how they would become self-sufficient in future and support parents during their old age. When the children become parents, they also, follow the same process of socialisation and expect the same pattern of behaviour from their children. Thus, mutual reciprocity between the aged and the young is quite essential for the sake of leading life safely and enjoying the god-given precious life peacefully. This, of course, does not always happen as a practice of 'give and take' process or as an instance of social security or social insurance rather it happens quite naturally for the parents who nourished and educated their children without any intention of getting any service from their children during their old-age.

From the very beginning of birth, the human children are tied down with their parents or grandparents intrinsically and remember for ever their love and affection and the warmth of their mother's breasts as a yardstick of their life. They experience it in a sustained eternal state of mind that brings them up into the main sphere of their life. So, when they become adult, as social beings and as responsible entities of the family or of the society, they respect their elders, obey them and acknowledge their authority both at the household as well as at the wider level of the society. Deviance of the younger people from this is not normally appreciated by the Indian tradition in traditional societies. In this regard Kautilya in his *Arthashastra,* has reprimanded those who neglect their aged parents and has permitted the village elders to punish those sons who fail to provide care for the aged parents (Nagesh, 1992: 280-281). Hence, it has been a trend and social practice since remote past to look after the aged; both in the Indian as well as in western societies. Coleman and Cressey have rightly pointed out that "In traditional societies with extended family system, increasing age is usually accompanied by increasing prestige" (1980-238). They also cite an example of traditional Chinese culture and say that "In the ancient Chinese family the eldest male held the lion's share of power. He was treated with reverence and respect, and even worshipped after his death. With the breakup of the extended family in western culture, the status of elders has suffered a severe decline" (*ibid*). In India, the case is also exactly the same in traditional societies. But if we consider the independence year as a cut off line, one can clearly differentiate the status of the aged in pre and post-independence Indian societies and comprehensively visualise how the status of these people is declining steadily over the past few decades after independence. After India achieved her independence, the process of modernisation took its high momentum, scope of white-collar jobs increased, mobility of people went up and women were empowered. All these factors together with other similar ones centred a drastic indirect impact on the aged and their social status reduced to a considerable extent and they are not suffering from a number of social and other problems in the fast changing societies. Some of the cardinal problems which these people now face may be noted as follows:

*(a)* Disintegration of the joint family/extended family system and shifting of authority from the older to the younger generation, i.e., from father to son;

*(b)* Development of individualistic nature of living, i.e., rise of nuclear family and attitudinal changes among the younger generation, thereby reducing social security for the aged;

*(c)* Dissimilar thinking, ideological clash and development of conflicting situations between generations;

*(d)* Reduction of social status to the secondary or even tertiary level in the family and also in the society;

*(e)* Leading a life of isolation with meagre or no income;

*(f)* Suffering from age-based diseases, lack of treatment and nursing facility by the household members etc.

When the case of the retired public servants residing on the outskirts of urban centres are dealt with, even if they are financially better off than those who were dependent on agriculture, running petty business, or employed in private sectors, their freedom is most often curtailed by the younger generation. They also face a number of other problems. Some of the important and basic problems are as follows:

*(a)* That in many cases their importance suddenly declines in the family after retirement;

*(b)* That the gratuity received after retirement is immediately spent either for the development of the house or utilised for the employment or rehabilitation purpose of unemployed children or is utilised in unproductive sectors under the absolute authoritarian management of the younger generation;

(c) That the monthly pension is either spent for the day-to-day household requirement under the imperative authority of the younger generation or in consultation with the pensioners or family pension holders;

(d) That disagreement of the pensioners or family-pension holders with the younger generation about utilisation of monthly pension according to the choice of the latter often create unfavourable situations in the family;

(e) That in many cases the pensioners or the family-pension holders do not get their favourite food items or proteinous diet for consumption even if they earn. It happens so more in case of those who have more grandchildren;

(f) That they face many problems to come over to urban centres for drawing pension or family-pension;

(g) That most of the middle class retired persons like to spend their retired life in their native villages but their children do not like to live in village homes. As a result, the aged are forced to lead solidarity life in villages and adjust themselves with the challenging situations. In the later stage when they fall ill, they do not get adequate care from their children who stay outside or in urban centres.

Thus, from the above discussion it can be educed that the senior citizens of Indian society as a whole face various problems which are conditional to different situations and also are age and culture based. Their problems are also greatly influenced by the fast changing social system in the post-independence period of modern India.

**Aging—A Conceptual Framework**

Aging is a natural process of becoming older and older. It is a universal reality. It is defined in different ways by different authors.

According to Tibbitts, "Aging is the survival of a growing number of people who have completed the traditional adult roles of making a living and child rearing and the years following the completion of these tasks represented as extension of life" (1966: 4).

Hess defines aging as "an inevitable and irreversible biological process of life (1976: 11-12).

Halder views that "Aging is the deterioration of a mature organism resulting from time-dependence, essentially irreversible changes intrinsic to all members of the species, such that, with the passage of time, they become increasingly unable to cope with the stresses of environment, thereby increasing the probability of death's (1960-26).

Aging, as defined by Jarry and Jarry in collins dictionary of Sociology is "the chronological process of growing physically older. However, there is also a social dimension in which chronology is less important than the meaning attached to the process. Different cultural values and social expectations apply according to gender and age group, and therefore there are socially structured variations in the personal experience of aging" (1995: 9-10).

Muttagi has described aging as a multi dimensional process and specifies that aging in its demographic sense is not the same as the biological process of aging which is dynamic and continuous. Chronological age does not measure physiological and psychological age. He further views that aging is generally associated with fatigue, decline in functional capacity of organs of the body, decrease of ability to cope with the stress of disease of trauma (1997: 8-9).

Generally speaking 'aging' has three broad dimensions and each one is associated with another. These are: (i) physiological aging, (ii) psychological aging and (iii) social aging.

**(i) Physiological Aging**

Physiological aging is the product of biological process. It is a process by which physical and mental changes occur through growth and decline. In the early years of life, 'growth' predominates and in the later years 'decline' predominates. (cf. Bhatia, 1993: 3) Generally the changes that occur in physiological aging is visual or phenotypic. So an 'aged' is easily identified out of its physical appearance as in old age skin is wrinkled, head and body hair becomes grey, tooth falls, etc. Apart from these visual changes, some other changes also occur inside the body which are not visual. Rao has pointed out that in old age the immunological system, cardiovascular system, digestive system, nervous system, endocrine system, reproductive system, skeletal system, respiratory system and function of kidney deteriorate (1994: 15-29).

**(ii) Psychological Aging**

Psychological aging is a process by which a person loses its mental ability. Most of ten psychological pressure or disturbances bring young people to look aged and it is reflected in body as an unnatural process. Poplin says that "one of the major problems of aging persons is the shock of growing old". He further points out that "we are ' 'aging' may be the *most profound shock* we experience in our lifetime" (1978: 339). This 'shock' of course hardens the remaining life course and the persons get older much faster than the natural process because of this psychological trauma attached to the person.

Wechsler states that "psychological capacities may show decline with age, but traits like interpretation and imagination may decline very little over the years" (1995: 275).

**(iii) Social Aging**

Social aging is a process by which a person acquires the superior knowledge and takes up responsible roles depending upon its age-status in the society. Relating to this, Bhatia says that "Every society has its own conception of aging and age groupings. Through the process of socialisation, the society ensures the transmission of social and cultural values from one generation to the next and enables its members to acquire necessary skills, values, norms etc. As the individual moves from one age-grade to the next, he acquires new roles in accordance with the prevailing practices. Age related roles, privileges and expectations are defined by the society. 'Social aging, as distinct from biological and psychological aging, thus, refers to the stage in the life span of the individual that is regarded as old age by the group" (1983: 5).

Muttagi says that it is very difficult to define social aging but he professes that social aging is administratively determined for purposes of social security, retirement from job in the organised sector, or for demographic classification, its consequences on the individual and community (1997: 9).

**Aged—Who are they?**

Since 'aging' is a process, it is very difficult to define the term 'aged'. There is no single definition which is unanimously accepted worldwide. When a 15-years-old considers a 30-year-old man aged, the latter treats a 50-year-old man aged and so on so forth. So, there is no clear cut definition as to whom we can consider aged. In this context, giving an example, Poplin says that "A 55-year-old person is 'old' to a 15-year-old but 'young' to an 80-year-old person. And all of us have known people who are 'old' at 40 and others are still 'young' at 75. Chronological age is often a poor criterion for distinguishing between the young and the old. The old are those people society categorises as old' (1978: 330). Atchey also points out that it is not easy to distinguish between the young and the old (1972: 6-8). But according to the Collin's dictionary of sociology, it is the last part of the individual's life course, associated with declining faculties, low social worth and detachment from previous social commitments. It is a social construct rather than a biological stage, since its onset signifies very historically and culturally (Jarry and Jarry, 1995: 460).

But of course, there is not a single age-specification which is accepted worldwide at which point a person could be treated as 'aged' or 'old' and thereby it would ensure retirement from the active life or from the main workforce. Different countries have set up different age specifications depending upon their development and average life expectancy of people. In western countries, persons aged 65 or above are normally considered 'aged' and are retired from jobs. Hence, Poplin defines persons aged 65 or more as 'old' as most of the companies require their employees to retire at this age. And this is the age when they become entitled to have full benefits of social security (1978: 330-331).

In India, the age of retirement varies from 55-65 years (Muttagi, 1997: 9) depending upon professional and nature of employing bodies. But, generally in most of the cases, the persons aged 60 years retire from Government of India jobs. However, there are many states including the state of Orissa, who have fixed up 58 years as the landmark-age for considering a person 'old' or 'aged' who are officially withdrawn from the main workforce and assume new roles in different social order and hence acquire a different social status in the household as well as in the society. But for the sake a administrative convenience and also for some other reasons 60 years is considered to identify a person as 'old' or 'aged' in census surveys made by Government of India.

### Working Definition of 'Aged'

The present study is primarily based on the data relating to the retired government employees in the state of Orissa. So, in most of the cases the employees of the government retire at the age of 58. In the present study, this age specification has been considered as a cut off point for considering a person 'aged'.

### Objectives of the Study

The broad objectives of the study are to find out the major socio-economic problems of the aged, particularly the retired government employees or pensioners and some others or non-pensioners. However, the specific objectives and seven fold. They are:

*(i)* to find out the living arrangement of the old after retirement from the formal organisations;

*(ii)* to analyse the attitudinal behaviour and the degree of social relationship between the old and the younger generation in the family and the process of social adjustment of the old after retirement;

*(iii)* to analyse the generation gap and decision-making process at the household as well as at the community level;

*(iv)* to find out the nature of work participation and economic viability of the old for maintenance of their household;

*(v)* to examine the mode of leisure and recreational activities of the old;

*(vi)* to examine the health status, treatment of diseases and mode if expenditure pattern on treatment; and

*(vii)* to find out the extent of problems relating to the official transaction of pension disbursement.

**The Universe**

The Universe of the study includes three broad groups of 'aged' who reside in 21 fringe multi-caste Hindu villages located around Bhubaneswar city. These villages belong to two different blocks namely Balianta and Bhubaneswar of the district of Khurda of Orissa.

The first group of 'aged' includes the pensioners and their spouses and the second group includes the non-pensioners and their spouses. The third group constitute the family-pension holders.

The aged population of these three categories constitute a total number of 148 persons of which 67 (45.27%) are men and the rest 81 (54.73%) are women. Of the 67 aged men, 55 (82.09%) are retired pensioners and the rest 12 (17.91%) constitute those who are retired from private organisations (3 or 4.48%), business sector (3 or 4.48%), agricultural sector (3 or 4.48%), and wage-earning sector (3 or 4.48%). And of the 81 aged women, 55 or 70.37 per cent are housewives, 21 or 25.93 per cent are family-pension holders and the rest 3 or 3.71 persons belong to wage-earning category.

**Methodology and Use of Tools**

The study has made use of various methods like village census survey, personal interview with informants through recording of information with the help of interview schedules. Besides, a questionnaire with close and open ended questions (Appendix: 1) was also administered and documentation of case studies was done. Observation method was followed while interviewing the informants during the course of the fieldwork.

Depending upon the objectives and the nature of the study, first of all the caste Hindu villages on the fringes of the Bhubaneswar city were selected purposively and retired persons and the family-pension holders in such villages were identified. Priority was given to cover almost all the retired persons and family-pensions holders. The non-pension holding 'aged' were selected on the basis of simple random method from within the sample villages.

Interviewing the aged on familial and other such social issues in front of the family members would be embarrassing. So, as far as possible, much precaution was taken to avoid such situations. The subjects were interviewed in conductive environments where they felt free to express their views, feelings, opinions and also suggestions. But surprisingly, in a sizeable cases the family members, particularly the daughters-in-law become very suspicious to their parents-in-law as if they would speak something against them. Thus, in such cases they intentionally tried to disturb the interviewer and the interview once and again by repeated personal appearance at the place of discussion. Even in some cases they constantly stood before the interviewer and instructed their parents-in-law not to disclose their family matters or speak out the truth. In such cases, the interviewer had to politely interfere in the matter to make the environment conductive to the farthest possible extent and in most of the cases the old persons fully cooperated with the interviewers to fulfil the purpose.

**Review of Literature**

Studying the problems of the aged as a separate branch of knowledge of social problems has been well recognised in western countries since early nineteenth century. But it was considered as such in India only in mid-post independence period. Bhatia writes that the problem of the aged in India was accepted and academically recognised in late 1960s when the "Indian Gerontological Association' was established by a group of young and enthusiastic scientists belonging to different branches of knowledge (1983: 13). Thus, this part of knowledge was almost untouched until early 1970s and hence, the studies which are not available in academic sphere had been primarily conducted during the last three decades.

Srivastava (1994) has studied a total number of 270 retired government employees consisting of 24 class-I, 48 class-II, 159 class-III, and the rest 39 class-IV aged persons. He has considered the age of 55 as a demarcating line for considering a person 'aged' as the retirement age varies from 55 to 58 years depending upon government stipulation.

His study is an exploratory one and he has aimed at gaining an insight knowledge as to how the retired persons of three districts, namely, Gorakhpur, Basti, and Deoria in the state of U.P., socially, economically, Psychologically and culturally adjust themselves with the changing situations. He has also pointed out some peculiar problems of these people, that is, as to how they view and manage to face the problematic situations either by themselves or with the help from government or NGOs.

Joseph (1991) has conducted a psychological study in terms of problems and personality of the aged in the district of Kottayam, in the state of Kerala. For the purpose of his study, he has considered a person of 60 years of age as 'old'.

He says that a paltry sum of pension is associated with poor living condition and suffering. Thus occupational insecurity, lack of training facilities and shortage of psychiatric and psychological services etc. are some of the main inadequacies in some of the advanced social systems of the world.

He has made a comparative survey between the home-living 'old' and the institutionalised 'old' and pointed out multiple problems, on physical, mental, economic, religious and occupational levels. Further he has also attempted to examine the attitude of the young (in between 20-50 years of age) towards the aged and has studied the personality of the aged in terms of certain selected personality variables. He finds that the young in Kerala do not have a negative attitude towards the old. Their attitude is clearly positive in nature and hence not discriminatory.

Kumar (1991) studies 460 old in the district of Chittoor in the state of Andhra Pradesh. He has taken 50 per cent of his sample from 2 urban centres, viz., Tirupati and Chittoor and the rest 50 per cent from 30 rural villages located within 30 kilometers distance from these two townships of the state. He has highlighted the family life and living arrangement of the old, delineated the interpersonal relations of the old and the changes which took place because of the operation of some forces like moderanisation, urbanisation etc., and also has described the familial, socio-economic, psychological and health problems of these people.

Sharma and Dak (1987) have edited a book on the purpose of aging in India and the socio-psychological problems attached to this process. Their work is a product of Joint Ventureship of Help-age India and the Department of Sociology, Haryana Agricultural University, Hissar.

The edition contains a total number of 23 short research papers authored by 37 workers. These papers are based on 3 broad categorises of problem. They are as follows:

*(i)* aging and the changing society,

*(ii)* socio-psychological problems of the aged, and

*(iii)* health and medical aspects of aging.

Broadly this volume explains about the modern forces, like education, urbanisation and industrialisation leading the disintegration of joint family system and development of materialistic and individualistic attitude or outlook of the younger generation, migration to cities and the effect of all these on the life style of the aged in India.

Kohli (1996) has studied the aged in India under a sponsored research project by Ministry of Welfare, Government of India, basing on the data available in census reports and National Sample Survey Organisation. He has analysed the demographic aspects of the aged, socio-economic and educational status of the aged as revealed in various surveys, family support system, health condition and socio-psychological adjustment in the new social environments.

Bhatia (1983) has comprehensively studied the living pattern, economic life, inter-personal relations, status and influence structure prevailing in family, health condition, religious behaviour, leisure time activities, and social participation in community affairs. His universe includes the public retired servants settled within the municipal limits of Udaipur city after retirement. He has stratified his universe into two groups, like gazetted and non-gazetted and has attempted to show the difference in the above variables.

Pati and Jena (1989) have edited a volume on the problems of the aged belonging to various states of India. It contains a total number of 27 articles prepared by various authors. Broadly this volume explains about different dimensions of the aged; particularly health and disease, demography, inter-generational support, work participation of the aged etc. and the role of the NGO sectors for the welfare of these people.

Mohanty (1989) has prepared a paper on retired government servants and their problems of socio-psychological adjustment as a theoretical base-line information. The author has vividly highlighted the financial, health, socio-psychological problems of these people. He has also pointed out the problems associated for utilising leisure time.

Dandekar (1996) has done a work on the elderly people of India. Basing on about 50,000 sample households, she has tried to differentiate the problems pertaining to regional variations between the rural and urban based old people of India on some specific sectors like health, financial constraint and role and function of old-age-homes. She has also evaluated the efficacy of the existing pension schemes and also suggests some remedial measures to overcome the loopholes. She has come to a point and says that the old-age-homes may offer a viable solution to the problems affecting the urban old, particularly poverty, shortage of housing, and often the harsh conflicting situations between young and old generations. She argues that since three-fourths of the aged people of India reside in rural bases, the major thrust of the welfare programmes and policies be directed at providing old-age-pensions. This, according to her, is not because the rural-aged are both well-integrated with their social milieu and not favourably disposed towards living in old-age-homes.

Muttagi (1997) carried out a study that speaks about problems of the aged both in developed and also in developing countries and examines how the welfare programmes and policies of the developed countries can be used as models for the developing countries. Further, he also examines the prevailing practices for the welfare programmes of the aged in India and how to improve these programmes depending upon the specific culture based problems.

Khan (1997) has surveyed the work of 22 voluntary organisations based in Delhi and outside Delhi which are engaged in the welfare of the aged in India. Basically he has studied the old, aged 60 or above with the help of secondary source data and information in order to find out the general problems faced by them and to examine the welfare measures taken up by these organisations and the day-care centres as well as to outline the direction at which the day-care centres may take to meet the existing and future service needs for the aged.

He has pointed out the health, economic and social problems of these people and also focussed on the social security, the process of public assistance and the institutional care. Finally, he suggests some constructive measures for the betterment of the aged through some modified roles of NGO sectors.

Muthayya and Aneesuddin (1997) have studied the rural aged in Andhra Pradesh and suggests interventions of the government and NGO sectors.

They have pointed out the socio-economic characteristics, health condition and dietary pattern, social life, recreation, past activities, hopes and worries of the old apart from pointing out the role and position of some inmates of the old-age-homes.

Raja (1997) has conducted a study on the aged, their problems and their future outlook in the state of Tamil Nadu under a sponsored project by the Ministry of Welfare, Government of India.

He has primarily shown the living condition of the aged who are above 60 years of age, their status in the household, the factors which influence the process of aging, socio-economic and health conditions, attitude of the aged towards family and the society, and also the mechanism of coping of the aged within the family and also in the community.

**Significance, Scope and Limitations of the Study**

It is noted earlier that the gerontological studies in social sciences, particularly in anthropological perspectives are very few in India. This branch of knowledge was almost an untouched part of research until late 1960s. However, after this period, quite a good number of work have been undertaken by various researchers in different parts of our country. But unfortunately, in Orissa, the number of studies made on this branch of knowledge is very limited. And hence, the status of the 'aged' in the state is very slightly known to all of us. More specifically the changing social status of the aged, particularly the pensioners and the family-pension holders living in the fringe villages of the cities of our state is quite unknown and no significant work has yet been done to show as to how urban life style among the younger generation affects the social status of the aged living in the proximity of urban centres. So, from this view point, this work not only highlights the social problems of the aged in the present context, but also going to indicate some measures, both according to the view point of the informants and also from the perspectives of the present piece of research. Hence, this study would be a useful document for researchers, academicians, students, administrators, NGOs and all those who are interested in the welfare of the aged in the State or elsewhere in the country. Still then there are some limitations of the study which may be noted as follows:

(*i*) that the study is based on a limited sample, and the fieldwork has been completed within a short period of time, and

(*ii*) however, the results of the study can be generalised to have some knowledge as regards the condition of the aged in the middle class households of Orissa, both in rural and semi-urban areas of the state.

**Module of Arrangement of Data**

In order to have a holistic idea about the problems and status of the aged in rapidly changing Indian society in general and in semi-urban context in particular, the result of the present study in presented in seven chapters.

The first chapter analysis the problems of the aged in Indian context and discusses the methodological aspects of the study. The second chapter shows the growth trend of the aged in India and in the state of Orissa over last few decades; more particularly after independence when the country experienced steady technological upgradation in medical science and how upgraded medical facilities and medical care reached to more and more people at individual level, which primarily caused enhancement of the life expectancy of Indian people. The next chapter contains some basic demographic features and socio-economic aspects of the study villages. The main thrust of the study comes in the next two succeeding chapters. When the fourth chapter describes about the demographic and socio-economic background of the aged economic contribution of the aged, generation gap and involvement of the aged in the decision-making process at household and community levels, the nature of their work participation and extent of contribution of physical labour, mode of utilisation of leisure time, their health status and treatment of diseases etc. The sixth chapter explains about the welfare measures and constitutional provisions available for the aged and suggestions of some comprehensive measures for the betterment and welfare of these people. The concluding or the seventh chapter summarises the findings of the study.

2

# Demographic Profile of the Aged in India and Orissa

### Life Expectancy at Birth and at the Age of 60

Over the years, proportion of the population aged 60+ to the social population is increasing very fast, both in developed and in developing countries of the world. It has been possible because of tremendous improvement in medical facilities, provision of higher quality of health services, increase in the economic status of the people and betterment in nourishment level. Altogether these factors have reduced the birth rate, lowered the rate of infant mortality and steadily increased the life expectancy of people in many countries. But with the increase in life expectancy, their problems are also increasing very fast coinciding with their higher longevity of life. If this can be tackled with the pace of development, the aged would enjoy their life peacefully, that would perhaps further increase their life expectancy.

In India, the life expectancy and the proportion of the aged is steadily increasing since last few decades. Irrespective of sex, the average life expectancy at birth was only 41.25 years in 1951-60 but it increased to 59.25 years in 1989-93 (Table: 2.1). As per the latest survey made by the Director General of Help-Age India, it is now 68 years for a general citizen of our country (The Samaj, 1998: 8). Likewise, the average life expectancy of an ordinary Indian irrespective of sex at the age of 60 has also increased from 12.4 years in 1951-60 to 15.55 years in 1989-93 (Table: 2.1).

Table 2.1 also shows in the life expectancy both at birth and at the age of 60. In all, during the four-survey years, viz, from 1951-60 to 1976-80, the life expectancy of males was slightly higher than the females but in the latter survey years, viz, from 1981-85 to 1989-93, the trend has just reversed. But what surprising is that beginning from 1951-60 to 1989-93, during all the survey years, the life expectancy of the female population at the age of 60 is witnessed to be more than those of the females.

**Percentage and Decadal Growth Rate of Aged in India and Orissa**

The percentage of population aged 60+ by sex in India is set out in Table 2.2. The concerned data for Orissa is presented in Table 2.3.

Table 2.2. delineates that in 1961 census, the percentage of aged to the total population was 5.58. But it increased to 5.97 in 1971, 6.49 in 1981 and 6.70 in 1991. The corresponding figures for the state of Orissa seem to be more or less same in the first three-census years which come to be 5.7 in 1961, 6.02 in 1971 and 6.39 in 1981. But surprisingly it is now 7. 20 in 1991 census (Table: 2.3).

However, if one compares the trend of the decadal growth rate of the aged population to the population of all age grades, it is found that in India, it was 32.32 per cent as against 24.88 per cent in 1961-71. It changed to 31.31 per cent as against 27.21 per cent in 1981-91 (Table: 2:4). But the data presented in Table 2.5 shows that the decadal growth rate of the aged population in Orissa was 32.93 per cent as against only 25.65 per cent of the total population in 1961-71. It increased to 35.37 per cent as against 20.06 per cent of the total population in 1981-91. Thus, the decadal growth rates of the aged population of both India and Orissa are found to have been much higher than the growth rate occurred among the total population.

**Dependency Ratio of the Aged in India and Orissa**

Dependency ratio is an important aspect of demographic studies. It speaks about the proportion of the children in the age group of 0-14 years and population aged 60 or more who depend on the working population falling within the age group of 15-59. But if the child population, i.e., 0-14 is deducted from the total population and then the dependency ratio of the aged is worked out, specifically it reflects their dependency on the working population.

Since the growth rate of the aged population is steadily increasing, the dependency ratio is also likely to show a similar trend. When one looks into the data available in Table 2.6, it comes to the notice that in 1961 the dependency ratio of the aged irrespective of sex was 10.93 in India. It increased to 12.26 in the last census year, i.e., 1991. But in Orissa, it was 9.30 in 1961 that comes to 10.81 in 1981 census (Table: 2.7).

**Sex Ratio of the Aged in India and Orissa**

Sex ratio indicates the proportion of females per 1000 males. The related statistics are presented in Table 2.8.

Irrespective of age, in India, the sex ratio was 940.94 in 1961 as against 1000.87 in Orissa. But it has come down to 926.79 as against 970.83 for Orissa in 1991 census. However, if the sex ratio of the population aged 60+ is considered, it seems that it was much higher compared to the sex ratio of the whole population of India as well as in Orissa during 1961. However, even though, over the years it has sufficiently reduced, in 1991, the sex ratio in the population aged 60+ has almost equal with that of the total population in India and Orissa. Still the sex ratio of the aged population in Orissa is found to be much higher (978.12) than India (930.31) as has been presented in the said table.

A balanced sex ratio is requested in all age groups; more particularly in the age group of 60+. It helps for having balanced mutual reciprocity between sexes; more so between spouses. But, it is perhaps because of the biological or any other such factors, the life expectancy of males and females do not coincide with each other. As a result of this, sex ratio fluctuates drastically in older age groups.

As shown as in Table 2.1, at the age of 60 years, for the males, the life expectancy was 11.8 year as against 13.00 years of the females in 1951-60. But in 1989-93 it increased to 14.9 years for males as against 16.2 years for the females. In other survey years females also showed a constant higher longevity of life over males.

This apparently signifies that the males are fortunate enough to get the socio-psychological support of their spouses during their old age or before they die. But unfortunately, the females are to spend their last part of life without their husbands and hence perhaps in a difficult state of mind and social situation.

**Table—2.1: Life expectancy at birth and at the age of 60 in India (1951-60 to 1989-93)**

| | *At birth* | | | *At 60* | | |
|---|---|---|---|---|---|---|
| *Period* | *Male* | *Female* | *Average* | *Male* | *Female* | *Average* |
| 1951-60 | 41.9 | 40.6 | 41.25 | 11.8 | 13.0 | 12.4 |
| 1961-70 | 47.1 | 45.6 | 43.35 | 13.0 | 13.4 | 13.2 |
| 1970-75 | 50.5 | 49.0 | 49.75 | 13.4 | 14.3 | 13.35 |
| 1976-80 | 52.5 | 52.1 | 52.3 | 14.1 | 15.9 | 15.0 |
| 1981-85 | 55.4 | 55.7 | 55.55 | 14.6 | 16.4 | 15.5 |
| 1986-88 | 57.0 | 57.4 | 57.2 | – | – | – |
| 1986-90 | 57.7 | 58.1 | 57.90 | 14.7 | 16.1 | 15.4 |
| 1987-91 | 58.71 | 58.6 | 58.35 | 15.3 | 16.2 | 15.25 |
| 1988-92 | 58.6 | 59.0 | 58.80 | 15.3 | 16.0 | 15.65 |
| 1989-93 | 59.0 | 59.7 | 59.37 | 14.9 | 16.2 | 15.55 |

*Note:* Data from 1987-91 to 1989-93 excludes Jammu & Kashmir & Mizoram.

*Sources:* Census of India for the period 1951-60 & 1961-70, 1986-88 and Sample Registration for the rest periods as published (expecting col. nos. 4 & 7) in Research and Development Journal of Help-age India in a paper prepared by Dr. M. Vijayanunni, Registrar General and Census Commissioner, India.

**Table—2.2: Percentage of population aged 60+ by sex in India (1961-1991)**

| Census year | All Ages | | | 60+ | | |
|---|---|---|---|---|---|---|
| | Total | Male | Female | Total | Male | Female |
| 1961 | 100.00 (438936918) | 100.00 (226146101) | 100.00 (212790817) | 5.58 (24712109) | 5.46 (12356687) | 5.71 (12355422) |
| 1971 | 100.00 (548159652) | 100.00 (284049276) | 100.00 (264110376) | 5.97 (32699731) | 5.94 (16874325) | 5.99 (15825406) |
| 1981 | 100.00 (665287849) | 100.00 (343930423) | 100.00 (321357426) | 6.49 (43167385) | 6.40 (22022869) | 6.58 (21144516) |
| 1991 | 100.00 (846302688) | 100.00 (439230458) | 100.00 (407072230) | 6.70 (56682000) | 6.69 (29364000) | 6.72 (27318000) |

*Note:*
1. Figures in brackets represent absolute number
2. 1961 figures excludes N.E.F.A., where all India Census Schedule was not canvassed, i.e., 297853 (P) 147100 (M) & 150753 (F).
3. 1981 figures excludes Assam and Jammu & Kashmir.
4. 1991 figures (all ages) includes projected figures of Jammu & Kashmir.
5. 1991 figures (60+) are extracted from the paper of Dr. M.Vijaynunni, Registrar General and Census Commissioner, India, as published in Research and Development Journal, a Periodical of Help-Age India.

*Source:* Census Report, Govt. of India.

**Table—2.3: Percentage of population aged 60+ in Orissa (1961-1991)**

| Census year | All ages | | | 60+ | | |
|---|---|---|---|---|---|---|
| | Total | Male | Female | Total | Male | Female |
| 1961 | 100.00<br>(17548846) | 100.00<br>(8770586) | 100.00<br>(8778260) | 5.7<br>(993979) | 5.15<br>(451313) | 6.18<br>(542666) |
| 1971 | 100.00<br>(21944615) | 100.00<br>(11041083) | 100.00<br>(10903532) | 6.02<br>(1321281) | 5.76<br>(636035) | 6.28<br>(685246) |
| 1981 | 100.00<br>(26370271) | 100.00<br>(13309786) | 100.00<br>(13060485) | 6.39<br>(1684929) | 6.13<br>(815729) | 6.66<br>(869200) |
| 1991 | 100.00<br>(31659736) | 100.00<br>(16064146) | 100.00<br>(15595590) | 7.21<br>(2280956) | 7.18<br>(1153090) | 7.23<br>(1127866) |

*Note:* Figures in brackets represent absolute number.

*Source:* Census reports, Govt. of India.

**Table—2.4: Decadal growth rates of population aged 60+ by sex in India (1961-71 to 1981-91)**

| Period | All ages | | | 60+ | | |
|---|---|---|---|---|---|---|
| | Total | Male | Female | Total | Male | Female |
| 1961-71 | 24.88 | 25.60 | 24.12 | 32.32 | 36.56 | 28.08 |
| 1971-81 | 21.37 | 21.08 | 21.68 | 32.01 | 30.51 | 33.61 |
| 1981-91 | 27.21 | 27.71 | 26.67 | 31.31 | 33.33 | 29.20 |

*Note:* Based on data available in Table 2.1.

**Table—2.5: Decadal growth rates of population aged 60+ by sex in Orissa (1961-1991)**

| Period | All ages | | | 60+ | | |
|---|---|---|---|---|---|---|
| | Total | Male | Female | Total | Male | Female |
| 1961-71 | 25.05 | 25.89 | 24.21 | 32.93 | 40.93 | 26.27 |
| 1971-81 | 20.17 | 20.55 | 19.78 | 27.52 | 28.25 | 26.84 |
| 1981-91 | 20.06 | 20.69 | 19.41 | 35.37 | 41.36 | 29.76 |

*Note:* Based on data available in Table 2.3.

*Source:* Census reports, Govt. of India.

**Table—2.6: Dependency ratio of population aged 60+ by sex in India (1961-1991)**

| Census year | Male | Female | Total |
|---|---|---|---|
| 1961 | 10.91 | 10.93 | 10.93 |
| 1971 | 11.39 | 11.47 | 11.47 |
| 1981 | 11.84 | 12.04 | 12.04 |
| 1991 | 12.16 | 12.16 | 12.26 |

*Source:* Census reports, Govt. of India.

**Table—2.7: Dependency ratio of population aged 60+ by sex in Orissa (1961-1991)**

| *Census year* | *Total* | *Male* | *Female* |
|---|---|---|---|
| 1961 | 9.30 | 8.48 | 10.11 |
| 1971 | 10.44 | 9.98 | 10.93 |
| 1981 | 10.59 | 10.11 | 11.08 |
| 1991 | – | – | – |

*Note:* 1991 figures could not be calculated as age-wise population is not yet available in census office, Bhubaneswar.

*Source:* Census Reports, Govt. of India.

**Table—2.8: Sex ratio among population aged 60+ in India and Orissa (1961-1991)**

| | *India* | | *Orissa* | |
|---|---|---|---|---|
| *Census* | *All age groups* | *60+* | *All age groups* | *60+* |
| 1961 | 940.94 | 999.09 | 1000.87 | 1202.42 |
| 1971 | 929.80 | 937.84 | 987.54 | 1077.37 |
| 1981 | 934.37 | 960.12 | 981.27 | 1065.55 |
| 1991 | 926.79 | 930.32 | 970.83 | 978.12 |

*Note:* Based on the data available in Table 2.5.

# 3

# Village Demography and Socio-Economic Profile

## Location of Study Villages

The study villages are located around the Bhubaneswar city. These are adjacent to its municipal boundary. But when all the study villages of Balianta block namely, Balianta, Satyabhamapur, Bhubanpur, Gotalgram, Garh Srirampur, Andilo, Tankapani, Bhainchua, Kantunia, Rahadamunda, Jasuapur and Indrapal are located on the eastern side of city along the river embankment of Bhargavi, the study villages of Bhubaneswar block, namely, Daruthenga and Chandaka are situated on the western side; Bikipur, Itipur, Jaipur, Nathpur, and Damodarpur on the southern side and Injena and Raghunathpur on the northern side.

## Household and Population Size

A detailed picture of village-wise household and population size is presented in Appendix No. 2. It is observed that when the village of Bhubanpur consists of highest number of households, i.e. 616, it is the village of Damodarpur that consists of minimum number of households which are only 24. But the village Bhainchua that consists of 542 households bears maximum population, which is found to be 3509. However, as the village Damodarpur shares the lowest number of households, it has also the lowest population size compared to rest of the study villages.

When the villages are categorised according to their household sizes, it is found that of the total 21 villages, maximum percentage (38.10) of village (8 nos.) have 301 or more households. There are 23.81 per cent or 5 villages that have 100 or less households (Table 3.1). The average household size per village comes to 269 (Appendix 2).

Regarding population size, it can be said that maximum percentage (28.57) or 6 villages have 2001 or more population. They are followed by 23.81 per cent or 5 villages having 501-1000 population, 19.05 per cent or 4 villages having 500 or less population and 14.29 per cent or 3 villages having 1501-2000 population (Table 3.2). The average population size per village comes to 1489.61 (Appendix 2).

**Caste Composition**

Caste composition is an important aspect of anthropological studies. It speaks about the functional characteristics of village institutions and provides socio-economic information of each individual of the village. As one caste has greater influence on the other, educational or economic status of person may be judged according to its caste. However, the role of castes have sufficiently been reduced during these days. But it cannot be redundant in the present day anthropological studies since caste seems to be still an essential component of village structure and is required to be studied to know the social background of individuals.

In this present study villages, Scheduled Castes (SCs) and Other Castes (OCs) are found in 85.71 per cent of villages. Scheduled Tribes (STs) are found only in 6 or 28.57 per cent of villages. Scheduled Tribes (STs) are found only in 6 or 28.57 per cent of villages (Table 3.3). If one looks into the data presented in Table 3.4, it comes to the notice that in 43 per cent or 9 villages, the proportion of Scheduled Castes is in between 21-40 per cent. It is less than 20 per cent in 6 or 28.57 per cent villages. There are about 2 (9.52%) villages which have 61 or more per cent of Scheduled Castes. However, the proportion of Scheduled Tribe population is 20 per cent or less than this in 4

(80.00%) villages of the total 5 villages having Scheduled Tribe population. The rest one village, however, constitutes Scheduled Tribe population that comes to be in between 41 to 60 per cent of the total population of the village.

So far as the castes other than Scheduled Castes and Scheduled Tribes are concerned, in case of maximum villages, i.e., 14 or 66.67 per cent, they constitute 61 or more per cent population (Table 3.4).

**Literacy**

Village-wise literacy is presented in Appendix No. 3. It points out that the literacy is maximum in case of the village Damodarpur which comes to 76.67 per cent. It may be due to its small composition of population. On the contrary Bhubanpur that constitutes the second highest population (2713) amongst the 21 study villages records lowest literacy which is merely 22.71 as against 49.09 per cent of the state (Appendix 3).

When the villages are grouped in various literacy ranges, it is observed that 12 or 57.14 per cent of villages record 41-60 per cent literacy and 3 or 14.29 per cent of villages have 61 or more people as literates (Table: 3.5).

**Table—3.1: Study villages according to No. of households**

| *Households* | *Total villages* | *% age to total study villages* |
|---|---|---|
| <100 | 5 | 23.81 |
| 101-200 | 4 | 19.05 |
| 201-300 | 1 | 4.76 |
| 301> | 8 | 38.10 |
| N.A. | 3 | 14.29 |
| **Total** | **21** | **100.00** |

*Note:* NA represents data not available in census records.

**Table—3.2: Study villages according to population size**

| *Population size* | *Total villages* | *% age to total study villages* |
|---|---|---|
| < 500 | 4 | 19.05 |
| 501-1000 | 5 | 23.81 |
| 1001-1500 | – | – |
| 1501-2000 | 3 | 14.29 |
| 2001> | 6 | 28.57 |
| N.A. | 3 | 14.29 |
| **Total** | **21** | **100.00** |

Note: As per Table 3.1.

**Table—3.3: Study villages according different communities (N = 21)**

| *Community* | *Total villages* | *% age to total study villages* |
|---|---|---|
| ST | 6 | 28.57 |
| SC | 18 | 85.71 |
| OC | 18 | 85.71 |
| NA | 3 | 14.29 |

Note: As per Table 3.1.

**Table—3.4: Proportion of ST, SC and OC population in study villages**

| Proportion | No. of villages | | |
|---|---|---|---|
| | *SC* | *ST* | *OC* |
| <20 | 28.57<br>(6) | 80.00<br>(4) | – |
| 21-40 | 42.86<br>(9) | – | 14.29<br>(3) |
| 41-60 | 4.76<br>(1) | 20.00<br>(1) | 4.76<br>(1) |
| 61> | 9.52<br>(2) | – | 66.67<br>(14) |
| N.A. | 14.29<br>(3) | – | 14.29<br>(3) |
| **Total** | **100.00<br>(21)** | **100.00<br>(5)** | **100.00<br>(21)** |

Note: As per Table 3.1.

**Table—3.5: Study villages according to proportion of literate persons**

| *Proportion (in % age)* | *Total villages* | *% age to total study villages* |
|---|---|---|
| <20 | – | |
| 21-40 | 3 | 14.29 |
| 41-60 | 12 | 57.14 |
| 61> | 3 | 14.29 |
| N.A. | 3 | 14.29 |
| **Total** | **21** | **100.00** |

Note: As per Table 3.1.

# 4

# Demographic Background of the Aged in Study Villages

Various social components altogether with economic condition and education of a person and his/her family members act as some of the important factors for determining the social status of an aged in both the patriarchal and matriarchal societies. However, more particularly age, sex, marital status, occupation, education, family structure etc. largely influence the socio-cultural and religious roles of individuals. Thus, these are considered as important social aspects for studying the inter-personal relationships within and outside the family. This, of course varies from culture to culture, religion to religion and even caste to caste. So, the social status of an aged person may differ in Brahman society from that of a different or a lower caste. Thus, with this background knowledge, we may now discuss the following demographic aspects of the aged under study. Basing on these aspects, the analytical part of the problems faced by these people could be dealt in the succeeding chapter.

### Distribution of Aged by Age and Sex

Table 4.1 shows the distribution of sample aged population by age and sex in five age grades, viz, 55-59, 60-64, 65-69, 70-74 and 75 and above.

There are 148 sample aged population in total which come out as a result of survey in 21 study villages. Of these, 67 or

45.27 per cent are of aged men and the rest 81 or 54.73 per cent are age women. Among the aged men, most (28.36%) are concentrated in the age grade of 60-64. Similarly this age grade also constitutes the highest proportion of aged women. But in this case, the percentage is as high as 37.04. So far as the total figures are concerned, the lowest age grade, i.e. 55-59 and the highest age grade, i.e., 75+ constitute more or less the same percentage of aged irrespective of sex. It comes to 12.16 per cent for the former age grade as against 12.84 per cent of the latter one. Hence these two age grades together constitute exactly 25 per cent of the total sample. The rest 75 per cent are concerned in the remaining 3 age grades, viz, 60-64 (33.11%), 65-69 (25.0%), and 70-74 (16.89%).

As per the recent survey made by Help-Age India, the average life expectancy of an ordinary Indian rests at the age of 68. Here, in this study we have not tried to show the exact number of sample old who are aged 68. This could not be possible because of the persistence of some limiting factors associated with formulation of the existing age grades. However, if the mid point of age grade of 65-69 is worked out to be 67.5 and is considered as the average life expectancy, then it comes to the notice that there are about 63 or 42.23 per cent of aged who have attained this age. The aged who are at the age of 70 or above constitute 44 persons irrespective of sex. They account for 29.73 per cent of the total sample size.

**Distribution of Aged by Caste and Sex**

Caste is an important social component of Indian Society. As such, it speaks of itself and identifies the social position of its members at the familial level and also at the level of society at the macro level of private life. In this context, acts as an important variable in determining the social identity of an individual.

As per the data available in Table 4.2, highest percentage of sample of either sexes belong to *Khandait* (warrior or militia) caste. It comes to 29 or 43.28 per cent for men as against 39 or 48.15 per cent of women in the sample. Next to them, more than 23 per cent of the sample belong to the *Karan* (scribe) caste; both men (23.88%) and women (24.69%). A significant proportion of the whole sample also belong to *Brahman* (priest) caste. But when it is 5 or 7.46 per cent for men, it is 6 or 7.41 per cent for women. However, if one looks at the total figures available in the same table, it comes to the notice that as many as 68 aged irrespective of sex belong to *Khandait* caste. They account for 45.95 per cent of the total sample of 148. They are followed by 36 or 24.32 per cent of aged belonging to *Karan* caste, 11 or 7.43 per cent belonging to *Brahman* caste, 8 or 5.41 per cent belonging to *Sundhi* (Alcohol seller) caste, 8 or 5.41 per cent belonging to *Teli* (oil crusher) caste, 3 or 2.03 per cent belonging to *Chasa* (agriculturist) caste, 2 or 1.35 per cent belonging to *Jyotish* (Astrologer) caste and 2 or 1.35 per cent belonging to *Kamara* (Blacksmith) caste.

### Distribution of Aged According to Material Status

Table 4.3 speaks about the marital status of the aged under study. In the total sample of 67 aged men and 81 aged women, 94.03 per cent of men are married as against 72.84 per cent of women. The rest have lost their respective spouses. Hence, they lead life without their life parents. Irrespective of sex, 82.43 per cent or 122 aged have their spouses as against 17.57 per cent or 26 aged who are either widows or widowers.

### Distribution of aged According to Occupation

Data relating to occupation of the aged is presented in Table 4.4. It reveals that of the total 67 aged men, 82.09 per cent or 55 are retired state government servants and hence draw pensions. (The last post held by these people is presented in Appendix 4). There are 3 or 4.48 per cent of aged men who were doing some jobs like yard-Gunner (1 or 33.33%) and sewing instructor (2 or 66.67%) in private sectors (Appendix 5). They do not get any pension as per the terms and conditions of their employing institutions. However, they had received some gratuity after their retirement. An equal number of aged men are there who were doing some petty business, like running of hotels (1 or 33.33%), vegetable vending (1 or 33.33%) and potato selling (1 or 33.33%) during their active life (Appendix 5). Similarly, 3 (4.48%) aged men were selling labour and were earning wages or are still earning their livelihood as wage-labour. As such their income is very meagre. However, from these 9 aged men, (business-3, agriculture-3 and wage earning-3), only 2 (22.22%) are now getting old-age pension from the state government through Panchayat Samities. But the amount of pension which has been fixed at Rs. 100/- per month per person is very meagre to sustain a person for a month as the cost of living has been very high and the inflation rate has reached its climax during these days.

So far as the occupation of the sample aged women is concerned, 57 or 70.37 per cent are housewives and 21 or 25.93 per cent are family-pension holders. The rest 3 or 3.71 per cent are wage-earners [Table 4.4 (b)]. Department-wise posts held by the deceased husbands of the family-pension holders are mentioned in Appendix 6. Only 1 (33.33%) aged woman, who works as a wage-earner, gets old-age pension from the local Panchayat Samiti.

**Distribution of Aged According to Occupation and Education**

Distribution of the aged according to their occupation and education is portrayed in Table 4.5. Among the pensioners, most (32.73%) of them are educated only upto primary level, i.e., from class I-V. They are followed by 23.64 per cent aged who have passed high school education, i.e., matriculation. But there are only 4 (7.27%) pensioners who have college education. Of these, 2 or 3.44 per cent of the total sample have completed intermediate level and the rest 2 or 3.44 per cent have completed graduation. Hence, educationally the pensioners are found to be very backward. This is because of the fact that during the studentship of these retired persons educational facilities were not available in rural areas as it is now.

The educational qualification of those aged men who were working in private sectors, running business, practising agriculture or working as wage-earners is confined to primary education only as not a single aged belonging to any of these categories is found to have passed high school certificate (HSC) examination or college education.

So far as the educational qualification of housewives or family-pension holders is concerned, nearby about 48 or 60 per cent are found to be illiterate. A total number of 10 or 12.35 per cent are educated in traditional non-formal educational institutions. However, there is only one aged woman who has passed intermediate examination; the first part of college students.

A further look at the same table reveals that of the total sample of 148, 50 or 33-78 per cent are illiterate. They are followed by 37 or 25 per cent of aged who have completed primary education. The percentage of those who have completed high school certificate examination comes to 8.78. There are only 5 (3.38%) aged who are having college education, viz, intermediate (2.03%) and graduation (1.35%).

**Distribution of Pensioners According to Government Service**

Table 4.6 describes that of a total of 55 pensioners, there are 39 persons who have served Government of Orissa capacities. They account for 70.91 per cent of the total sample; and of the rest of 16 (29.09) persons, one worked under the Union Government. The department-wise position held by the pensioners are available in Appendix 4.

**Distribution of Pensioners According to Class of Last Post Held**

So far as the class of the last post held by the pensioners is concerned, more than 55 per cent (56.33) of pensioners have retired from class-III jobs. They are followed by 38.18 per cent of pensioners who served as class-IV employees either in state or in Union Government and have now retired. The whole census constitutes only 3 pensioners who have retired from class II jobs. They account for 5.45 per cent of the total 55 pensioners (Table 4.7).

So far as the posts held by the deceased husbands of family-pension holders are concerned, there are 16 or 76.9 per cent of family-pension holders, whose deceased husbands had retired from class-IV jobs. In case of the case of the rest 5 or 23.81 per cent of women their deceased husbands were working as class-III employees either in State Government or in Union Government (Table 4.8).

**Distribution of Pensioners According to Age at Retirement**

Age at retirement differs from government to government and even post to post as here is no strict uniformity. In case of the Government of Orissa, 58th year is fixed for an employee to be retired. But it is normally 60 years in case of Union Government employees. However, this norm has changed from time to time in past.

In the present study, it is found that as many as 40 or 72.73 per cent pensioners have been retired at the age of 58. The pensioners who have retired at the age of 60, account for 12 persons of 21.82 per cent of the total 55 pensioners. The rest 3 or 5.45 per cent of pensioners are found to have been voluntary retirement before attaining 58 years of age either because of their ill health or because of rehabilitating their educated un-employed children.

**Table—4.1: Distribution of aged by age and sex**

| *Age group* | *Men* | *Women* | *Total* |
|---|---|---|---|
| 55-59 | 3 (4.48) | 15 (18.52) | 18 (12.16) |
| 60-64 | 19 (28.36) | 30 (37.04) | 49 (33.11) |
| 65-69 | 15 (22.39) | 22 (27.16) | 37 (25.0) |
| 70-74 | 18 (26.87) | 7 (8.64) | 25 (16.89) |
| 75+ | 12 (17.91) | 7 (8.64) | 19 (12.84) |
| **Total** | **67 (100.0)** | **81 (100.0)** | **148 (100.0)** |

*Note:* Figures in brackets represent % age.

**Table—4.2: Distribution of aged by caste and sex**

| *Caste* | *Men* | *Women* | *Total* |
|---|---|---|---|
| Brahmin (Priest) | 5 (7.46) | 6 (7.41) | 11 (7.43) |
| Chasa (Agriculturist) | 2 (2.99) | 1 (1.23) | 3 (2.03) |
| Gauda (Cattle breeder) | 5 (7.46) | 5 (6.17) | 10 (6.76) |
| Jyotish (Astrologer) | 1 (1.49) | 1 (1.23) | 2 (1.35) |
| Kamara (Blacksmith) | 1 (1.49) | 1 (1.23) | 2 (1.35) |
| Khandait (Warrior) | 29(43.28) | 39(48.15) | 68 (45.95) |
| Karan (Scribe) | 16(23.88) | 20(24.69) | 36 (24.32) |
| Sundhi (Trader of alcohol) | 4 (5.97) | 4 (4.94) | 8 (5.41) |
| Teli (Oil crusher) | 4 (5.97) | 4 (4.94) | 8 (5.41) |
| **Total** | **67(100.0)** | **81(100.0)** | **148(100.0)** |

*Note:* Figures in brackets represent % age.

**Table—4.3: Distribution of aged according to marital status**

| *Sample* | *Married* | *Widow/widower* | *Total* |
|---|---|---|---|
| Men | 63 (94.03) | 4 (5.97) | 67 (100.0) |
| Women | 59 (72.84) | 22 (27.16) | 81 (100.0) |
| **Total** | **122 (82.43)** | **26 (17.57)** | **148 (100.0)** |

*Note:* Figure in brackets represent % age.

**Table—4.4(a): Distribution of aged men according to occupation**

| *Occupation* | *Frequency* | *% age* |
|---|---|---|
| Retired pensioners (government service) | 55 | 82.09 |
| Retired from private organisations | 3 | 4.48 |
| Business | 3 | 4.48 |
| Agriculture | 3 | 4.48 |
| Wage-earning | 3 | 4.48 |
| **Total** | **67** | **100.0** |

**Table—4.4(b): Distribution of aged women according to occupation**

| *Occupation* | *Frequency* | *% age* |
|---|---|---|
| Housewives | 57 | 70.37 |
| Family-pension holders | 21 | 25.93 |
| Wage-earning | 3 | 3.71 |
| **Total** | **81** | **100.0** |

**Table—4.5: Distribution of aged according to occupation and education**

| *Occupation* | *Total sample* | *Illiterate* | *NFE* | *Primary* | *Middle* | *High school (under metric)* | *Metric* | *Intermediate* | *Graduation* |
|---|---|---|---|---|---|---|---|---|---|
| Pensioners | 55<br>(100.0) | 1<br>(1.82) | 4<br>(7.27) | 18<br>(32.73) | 9<br>(16.36) | 6<br>(10.91) | 13<br>(23.64) | 2<br>(3.64) | 2<br>(3.64) |
| Private job | 3<br>(100.0) | – | – | 1<br>(33.33) | 1<br>(33.33) | 1<br>(33.33) | – | – | – |
| Business | 3<br>(100.0) | – | 2<br>(66.67) | 1<br>(33.33) | – | – | – | – | – |
| Agriculture | 3<br>(100.0) | 1<br>(33.33) | 1<br>(33.33) | 1<br>(33.33) | | | | | |
| Wage-earning | 3<br>(100.0) | – | 3<br>(100.0) | – | | | | | |
| Housewife/ family-pension holders | 81<br>(100.0) | 48<br>(59.26) | 10<br>(12.35) | 16<br>(19.75) | 5<br>(6.17) | 1<br>(1.23) | – | 1<br>(1.23) | – |
| **Total** | **148**<br>**(100.0)** | **50**<br>**(33.78)** | **20**<br>**(13.51)** | **37**<br>**(25.0)** | **15**<br>**(10.14)** | **8**<br>**(5.41)** | **13**<br>**(8.78)** | **3**<br>**(2.03)** | **2**<br>**(1.35)** |

*Note:* Figures in brackets represent % age.

**Table—4.6: Distribution of pensioners according to government served**

| *Govt.* | *Frequency* | *% age* |
|---|---|---|
| State | 39 | 70.91 |
| Union | 16 | 29.09 |
| **Total** | **55** | **100.00** |

**Table—4.7: Distribution of pensioners according to class of last post held**

| *Class of the job* | *Frequency* | *% age* |
|---|---|---|
| II | 3 | 5.45 |
| III | 31 | 56.36 |
| IV | 21 | 38.18 |
| **Total** | **55** | **100.00** |

**Table—4.8: Distribution of family-pension holders according to class of post held by their husbands**

| *Class of job* | *Frequency* | *% age* |
|---|---|---|
| III | 5 | 23.81 |
| IV | 16 | 76.19 |
| **Total** | **21** | **100.00** |

**Table—4.9: Distribution of pensioners according to age at retirement**

| *Age at retirement* | *Frequency* | *% age* |
|---|---|---|
| 58 | 40 | 72.73 |
| 60 | 12 | 21.82 |
| <58* | 3 | 5.45 |
| **Total** | **55** | **100.00** |

*Note:* * represents those who have taken voluntary retirement.

5

# Social Situation and the Problems of the Aged

## Family Type and Living Arrangement of the Aged—Life Condition

One of the three basic necessities of human life is to have a house. It is not only required to protect oneself from sun, rain and cold but also to lead a safe and comfortable familial life. It facilitates a group-life and hence centres to a deep social bondage among the family members who may be married couples, parents, grandparents, uncles, aunts, nieces, nephew etc. This group-life ultimately provides social and economic security for one another. Hence, home and family are considered as correlated concepts. As a result, any one of these two cannot be properly understood without the help of the other. Therefore, so far as the social and economic securities of a person is concerned, first of all we are to deal with each of these two aspects, viz., family type and housing provision before we discuss the living condition of these people.

Discussion on the family types to which the aged belong becomes futile unless the basic characteristic features of the joint family system that has existed in India since long past as a unit of social and cultural bondage and economic constituent among the people in a joint family system all possible social, economic and moral support systems are inherently very important for the members. This support system is enjoyed by the people of a number of generations; both in vertical as well as in horizontal lines living jointly under the common roof. In a short, it can be said that joint family is a system of social insurance against old age and all forms of social, economic, psychological, physical weaknesses of the inmates.

It is very natural that when a person gets older and older, he/she becomes more and more afraid of his/her future security. But in a joint family system, he/she finds himself/herself quite safe and secured from social and economic view points as his/his authority in old age or even simple existence is highly respected, honoured and acknowledged by the juniors in the patrilineal and also in matrilineal societies in the interest of social status and prestige of the family. But now-a-days, joint family system has considerably lost its social importance and economic significance because of various reasons. In the urban fringes, the importance of this system is very steadily deteriorating because of industrialisation and also because of high pressure of moderanisation and other such related reasons. A sense of consumerism fast engulfing the younger generations.

However, this problem is not specific to any particular state or place rather it is very broad in its perspective. The state of Orissa is not an exception to it. The situation around Bhubaneswar, the state capital of Orissa, has become very grim as the younger people, specifically belonging to the first and second descending generations have become very individualistic, freedom loving, and city-oriented in nature. This has led to the decline of the sanctity of the joint family system and hence it is being disorganised, and is disintegrating at a faster pace than the other forms of family. Ultimately the old people fall prey to it and the consequences are becoming very alarming for all of us.

**Family Types of the Aged**

The data available in Table 5.1 indicate that of the total number of 148 aged, maximum, i.e., 69 or 49.62 per cent of them live in vertically extended families. Even though, sociologically the nature of extended families are more or less same with the joint family system, here the most important factors are: the provision of common property and concentration of authority system in one person, i.e., the eldest male of the house does not exist. As a result, the social standing of the aged members belonging to this type of family may not be regarded as encouraging or desirable. Next to them, quite a good number of aged are having nuclear families. They are followed by 27 or 18.24 per cent of aged who live in supplemented families. A total number of 2 (1.35%) belong to sub-nuclear family and the rest one (0.68 %) aged resides in a broken family.

**Number of Generations Living Together**

Association with the people of the same generation is natural to all the living creatures, especially the human beings. This is spontaneous as a regular attraction between persons belonging to the same generation or age grade and it automatically happens as per the law of the nature.

Within the family, the old people generally require the co-operation and friendship of their counterparts who may preferably be either the male spouse/s or female spouse/s. However, they also requires the help of members of filial generations. In this context data presented in Tables 5.2, 5.3 and 5.4 may be referred to. Table 5.2 reveals that a total number of 88 (44.46%) aged are living in families where the people of three generations, viz., ego, ego's son and wife and ego's son's children are available. They are followed by 43 or 29.05 per cent of aged who are staying with at least one generation, excluding themselves. The rest 17 or 11.49 per cent of aged stay alone.

If a further analysis is made, it can be observed from Table 5.3 that there are 26 or 17.57 per cent of aged persons in which cases they are living alone without a person of their own generation. These people may be widows or widowers. However, as may as 122 or 82.43 per cent of these people have people of their own generation. Ego, with its first descending generation constitute 129 cases. They account for 87.16 per cent of the total sample. The aged who are living with the kins of second descending generation come to be 87 in number. Their percentage is 58.78. There are only 2 (1.35%) aged who have some members of their 1st ascending generation.

**Aged Persons Living with Specific Consanguineal and Affinal Kins**

The living arrangement of the aged is not perspicuous unless the exact relationships of family members living together are known. So, here, an attempt has been made to point out such relationships of the members living together with the aged.

Of the total 148 aged, there are 17 (11.49%) aged (viz., 5 or 9.09 per cent of pensioners, 8 or 13.33 per cent of housewives, 2 or 66.67 per cent of old farmers, 1 or 33.33 per cent of old businessmen and 1 or 33.33 per cent of old wage-earner), who lead life only with their spouses. The social condition of these people is very pitiable since there is nobody to look after them in the event of illness or any exigency. However, apart from these, highest percentage, i.e., 37.84 or 56 persons live with their spouses, married sons and unmarried grandchildren. They are followed by 14.19 per cent or 21 aged who live along, i.e. without spouse but with married sons and unmarried grandchildren; 4.05 per cent or 6 persons with spouse and married son/s but without grandchildren; 3.38 per cent or 5 persons with spouse, married son/s and unmarried children (both son/s and daughter/s) and unmarried grandchildren; 1.35 per cent or 2 aged with spouse and unmarried grandchildren; 1.35 per cent or 2 aged with spouse, their parent/s and unmarried children of self; 1.35 per cent or 2 aged with spouse, unmarried children, daughter's unmarried children and wife's sister; 1.35 per cent or 2 aged alone (without spouse) with unmarried children etc. There is an old who is living with his spouse and unmarried children of his daughter. It happened so when the adopted son was separated from them after his marriage and their hopes were shattered. Another old man is also there who is very unfortunate. He has also his spouse and the only married son. Hence he is bound to live with the widow of his deceased son and his unmarried grandchildren. The rest one old person has lost her husband and hence living alone with her married and unmarried children and grandchildren.

**Availability of Living-Rooms and the Aged**

Housing is a major problem all over the rural India. It is more rampant among the people of low and middle income groups. In the present study we are concerned with the aged who belong to the middle class among the caste Hindu Oriya people. Housing is observed to be a great problem among these people.

The study shows that highest percentage (42.57) or 63 aged have only 2 living-rooms followed by 32.43 per cent who have 3 living-rooms. Nearly about 12 per cent own only a single living-room. Among the informants who possess 4 and 5 living-rooms, account for 10.14 and 3.32 per cent respectively and the rest one does not have any living-room (Table 5.5).

When a question like whether the available living-rooms are sufficient for all the family members was asked to the informants, about 40 per cent (39.86) of then gave a positive answer and the rest gave a negative answer (Table 5.6). A total number of 59 aged (39.86%) persons said that the available rooms at their disposal are sufficient for all the family members; and only about 34 per cent (33.90) of them have separate living-rooms and the rest 66 per cent do not have separate rooms. However, from amongst a total number of 89 aged who have opined that the available living-rooms are not sufficient, 13 (14.61%) have been fortunate enough to have separate living-rooms. This signifies that their children are very generous towards them. The total figures indicate that as a whole there are only 19.59 per cent or 29 aged who have separate living-rooms and the rest 80.41 per cent or 119 do not have the same.

Further, a cursory look at the Table 5.7 reveals the fact that comparatively a larger percentage (23.88) or 16 aged persons have separate living-rooms as against only 16.05 per cent or 13 aged women. This otherwise indicates that more aged women (83.95%) than aged men (76.12%) do not have living-rooms for their personal use and living. This is primarily because of the existing practice of male supremacy and the fact of persistence of gender discrimination. This fact becomes very conspicuous when many spontaneously say that the old women are adjustable in any room but certainly not the old men. In addition to this, there is also another factor which is an inherent conscientious character of Indian women in traditional patriarchal societies They feel subordinate to their men counterparts and hence relinquish all possible comforts to them not only because of their wifely devotion towards their husbands but also for earning ritual merits as per the traditional belief of Hindu social system.

When it was enquired into the fact that whether the aged have specific living-rooms for their personal use or not, it came to the fore that of the total 119, 45.38 per cent or 54 aged are adjusted in any room depending upon the situation. Next to them, about 30 per cent or 35 aged reside in the entrance-rooms which are normally used for a variety of purposes like storing of vehicles, foodgrains fuel wood etc. The condition of 21.85 per cent or 26 aged is found to be very miserable. They lead life in destitution or enclosed verandah. Hence they have very meagre space for their personal use. In most of the cases a cot is permanently set in the verandah and some sac screens or screens made of fronds are used for protecting them from sun, rain and cold. In this context the case study no. 2 may be referred to. The condition of the rest aged persons are found to be more serious as 2 or 1.68 per cent of them reside in abandoned cowsheds. But fortunately, they have larger space to use in such cowsheds. One person is found to be living in an enclosed verandah of its neighbour on request and the rest one spends his day time in his own house but he has to sleep in the premises of the village community house or *Bhagabat Ghar*[1], located within the village (Table: 5.8).

## Economic Support, Work Participation and Contribution of Physical Labour Towards Family

### Economic Contribution of the Aged

In many cases the aged people are considered as a social or an economic growth but in reality they are not so. From various view points they are very helpful to the family and their presence is essential for the well-being of the family or even the society as a whole. They render economic support, and physically participate in a number of day-to-day activities which also include participation in various arduous work, sometimes against their ill-health or will.

---

1 Village temple where Lord Krishna is generally worshipped. It is owned and maintained by the villagers or the members of a particular ward of the village.

The retired government servants and the family-pension holders contribute financial assistance directly in ready cash and hence their economic contribution to the family is very clearly distinct and significant. The other aged persons who may be housewives or non-pension holders also contribute financial help in one way or other but their help is not so distinct in so far as the contribution of ready cash is concerned. However, they try to compensate it by doing various day-to-day work either being conscious parents or because of their own interest so as to justify their experience and that the family members, particularly the earning heads must not consider them as economic burden.

In the above context one may refer to the data presented in Table 5.9, 5.10, 5.11, 5.12, 5.13 and 5.14. Data available in Table 5.9 reflect that there are 55 pensioners and 21 family-pension holders who earn ready cash as their pension at the end of every month. Irrespective of these aged people, maximum, i.e. 45 or 59.21 per cent of them earn between Rs. 1001/- Rs. 1500/- per month. Next to them there are 20 per cent (19.74) or 15 persons whose earnings are in the income slab of Rs. 1501/- to Rs. 2000/ -. They are followed by 7 (9.2%), 3 (3.95%), and 2 (2.64%) persons who earn in-between Rs. 2001/- to Rs. 2500/-, Rs. 3001/- or more, less than Rs. 1000 and Rs. 2501/- to Rs. 3000/- per month respectively. A further look at the same table reveals the fact that when the earning of the family-pension holders is restricted only within the income slab of Rs. 1501/- to Rs. 2000/-, it ranges upto Rs. 3001/- or more in case of the pensioners. Hence, the average per capita per month income of the family-pension holders is found to be lower than the pensioners which come to be Rs. 1389.52 in case of the formers as against Rs. 1843.73 of the pensioners (Table 5.10). The amount of pension of a retired person is substantially reduced to about 50 per cent when his/her spouse is dead.

**Expenditure Pattern of the Aged**

Expenditure pattern of the aged has a special characteristic feature since they are retired from the active life process and are not much involved in home management. It may be observed from the data presented in Table 5.11 that more than 76 per cent of family-pension holders hand over the total pension holders hand over the total pension amount to their sons for home management; but it is only 22 per cent of the pensioners who do so. About 51 per cent pensioners keep their pension with them, which they spend in the management of their household. This happens because they belong to a patriarchal society and in that case, they do not normally like to hand over the authority to son/s so long as they are active or until their authority is honoured by their son/s. The total figures reveal that a total number of 31 aged accounting for 40.79 per cent keep their whole pension with themselves and help in managing the household. But there are as many as 28 or 36.84 per cent who do not keep even a small portion of their income with themselves rather hand over the same to their son/s or whoever is the manager of home in descending order of authority. The rest 17 or 22.37 per cent, however, partly keep their income with themselves and the rest hand over to their son/s. Still then the part-income which they keep with themselves is also ultimately spent for the general purpose of the household as most of them opine that they cannot spend it for the interest of their own. However, keeping own income with self and spending it for the benefit of the family gives them an eternal pleasure which is not expressive outwardly.

**Work Pressure and Participation of Non-bedridden Aged in Daily Chores of Life**

In traditional caste Hindu society, there is job specification for each sex. It is known as the division of labour.

There is no society anywhere in the world, where a person is socially free to do any work irrespective of its gender as both in patriarchal and also in matriarchal societies, some works are women specific and some are men specific. Hence the work of a man is not ordinarily done by a woman. Similarly, a man does not like to perform such work which a woman should perform. If the system is broken by any person on choice, he/she is not respected or given due prestige in the society. However, these social norms become futile when a person is alone or leads a broken life or is pressurised out of any circumstance. In such a case, he/she may violate the norms and do nay work that is required for his/her smooth living or survival. Some of such persons may be aged men and women. In this case, an aged man may cook and even clean utensils or house floor even if these are specific to the lesser sex, i.e., women. However, in this context one may refer to the data available in Table 5.12 and 5.13.

It may be observed from the Table 5.12 that the aged men frequently help in 8 important day-to-day activities. The aged women have been seen rendering their physical labour in 9 such activities.

The important activities which the aged men frequently attend to, are: looking after domestic animals, like cattle (34.38%), supervision of agricultural work, like watching the employed wage-labourers (32.81%); attending relatives during social requirements, like birth and marriage ceremonies, death rituals etc. (31.25%); shopping (28.13%); looking after the education of grandchildren (26.56%), etc. There are also 1.56 per cent aged men who frequently cook their daily-food, clean utensils and house floors, wash clothes even if these works are generally done by the women; they are compelled to perform these works either because of their helpless condition or because there is no alternative left for them to manage these works otherwise.

So far as the work of the aged women is concerned, the most important work which they frequently do is: cleaning of utensils are house floor; it is done by 37.97 per cent of them. These aged women are followed by those who frequently cook daily-food (22.78%), work as baby-sitter (16.46%), supervise agricultural works (10.13%), look after the education of grandchildren (8.86%), look after the domestic animals (7.59%), wash clothes (6.33%), and attend to relatives during social events (3.80%).

If the aged men and women who are found to render their physical labour occasionally are added up with the figures concerning those who frequently do the above activities, a different picture comes into the fore which may be seen from the total figures available in the same table.

Supervision of agricultural work involves strenuous physical labour. So, this work is generally done by men but a total number of 16 or 20.25 per cent of them also do this job. Similarly looking after domestic animals is also a very painstaking work. It includes feeding the animals, cleaning their body, cleaning their sheds etc. As a result, this work is also specific to the male sex but practically there are more than 24 per cent aged women who do this work.

Cooking daily-food, cleaning utensils, and house floor and washing clothes mainly attended to by the woman. But there are 8 or 12.5 per cent of aged men who are engaged in cooking their daily-food and cleaning used utensils. Similarly there are 5 or 7.81 per cent of aged men who wash clothes. Hence, it can be concluded that when the age of a man or woman increases or when a person becomes old, his/her gender-based social status gradually reduces, which coincides with the increment of age. So, an aged, either engages himself/herself out of his/her own interest or is engaged in any work ignoring the sexual division labour because of the situational compulsion or their helpless condition.

However, even though there are many aged who undertake their day-to-day works out of their own interest, quite a large number of them are these who are either compelled to do such work because of their helpless condition. There are 42.82 per cent of aged who engage themselves in supervision of agricultural works out of their own interest as it provides them an engagement and gives pleasure. The rest are either compelled to do the work or do it because of the situation.

A total number of 30 or 57.69 per cent of aged look after the domestic animals out of their own interest. The rest, however, are compelled to do this work.

Cooking, cleaning of utensils and house floor, washing clothes etc., are some of the important aspects of daily life. A man expects these works to be done by their children, preferably by daughters or daughters-in-law. But there are 12 or 31.58 per cent, 37 or 60.68 per cent and 3 or 17.65 per cent of aged persons who cook, clean utensils and house floor and wash clothes respectively out of their own interest, and the rest do these work under compulsion.

Cooking is considered as a better or prestigious work than cleaning of soiled utensils. Both these works are tedious but physical labour is not ordinarily felt in cooking because of the social prestige involved in this work. As a result, many aged women let their daughters-in-law to cook daily-food and engage themselves in cleaning utensils spontaneously either for protecting the social prestige of their family or because of some other reasons. But most young ladies, preferably the daughters-in-law impose the work of cleaning utensils on their mother-in-law without properly understanding their mind. This ultimately creates a difference between the two and in course of time the relationship becomes very unpleasant.

Baby sitting to be an easy but practically it is an arduous work as it involves extensive moving and running after children. However, it is easy to look after infants as they are tiny. After all, this work gives much, pleasure to the grandparents, particularly to the grandmothers. So long as they are active, they do this work spontaneously. But when it is imposed on them against their ill-health or desire, they land in trouble. There are about 28 per cent of aged on whom this work is imposed. However, if the aged men or women do not work for any reason, they are ill-treated in various ways and in many cases the consequences become very bad for them. In some cases, they are denied their daily food or even separated from their sons. In this context one may refer the case study number 1, 4 and 7. However, it is observed from Table 5.14 that in 17.48 per cent of cases sons irritate or show their displeasure towards their aged parents who do not work as per the demand of the situation or neglect the work assigned to them. In 22.38 per cent of cases, daughters-in-law behave improperly towards their aged parents-in-law. If a cursory look is given at the data presented in the same table, a peculiar trend is observed. When 34.38 per cent of sons irritate on their aged fathers, it is only 7.81 per cent of daughters-in-law who do so on their fathers-in-law (Hu Fa). A reverse trend is observed for the aged women where 38.17 per cent of daughters-in-law irritate on their mothers-in-law (Ho Mo) and it is only 3.80 per cent of sons who react adversely towards their aged mothers.

### *Social Relationship with Family Members, Renderance of Consultancy Service and Involvement in Decision-Making Process and Household and Community Levels*

Man is a social being. He lives in society and keeps social relationship with his family members, kins, friends, and neighbours.

Establishment of institutionalised affinal relationship starts from the time of marriage, that is after a man and a woman are ritually tied with each other and begin their martial life. This social system is unique only to the human beings as it is not observed to have been there in this manner among any other living creatures of the world. Hence, an adult man and woman begin their conjugal relationship with each other from their marriage as husband and wife. This husband and wife relationship becomes very strong since it involves a deep socio-psychological attachment leading to love and sex between them. This relationship gives birth to offsprings for various social and biological needs. After the birth of children, the man becomes a father and the woman, a mother. The social bondage among these 3 types of persons, viz, ego, ego's spouse and ego's children or attachment between these two contiguous generations, viz, parent and children, becomes very strong and well organised as these persons are primary kins to each other who may be affinal or consanguineal.

In this sort of social bondage, each one of, them is dependent on the other in some way or other and hence the social requirements of one person becomes very essential for the well-being of the other. First of all, apart from satisfying sexual urge, a husband depends on his spouse for maintenance of his household work, like cooking, looking after children at home etc. On the other hands, wife depends on her husband for her livelihood. The children born to them require their nourishment for being brought up properly and safely. In return, the parents also expect their children should provide them old-age security and so on and so forth. Thus, each family member has some responsibility towards others and the equation of social requirement and dependence of different kins within the family is well balanced. As a result, negligence in duty of any kin is not generally appreciated by the family or by the society as a whole with a view to providing social and economic security to the farthest possible extent among the inmates of a family. This social system is age-old and prevalent in all human societies throughout the world. But with the passage of time, the people belonging to the younger generations, mostly filial or second descending generation are moving away from the basic motives of familial bondage or from their parents or grandparents at a very faster pace because of generational gap, ideological differences and egocentric clash between generations.

**Motives Behind Procreation of Children**

With a view to understand the field reality, in the present context, several questions (Appendix 1) of which most are of very sensitive type, were put to the aged men and women under study. First of all, when a question on the motives prevalent behind begetting of offsprings was put, some overlapping answers with very pinpointed social justification came out into the picture (Table 5.15). Highest Percentage of aged opined that they had procured children in order to get parenthood as it is very essential for a man or a woman. If a man or a woman is not able to produce a child, her social position in the society is considerably undermined. She is considered as an inauspicious person and the people do not like to see their faces in the morning or when they go out for attending to an important work, because it is believed that their appearance portents against success. Another aspect is that by becoming a parent one gets satisfaction of fullness of his/her own life.

Next to the above reason, nearly about 70 per cent or 103 aged person said that they had thought and desired to have old-age security from the children which led them to beget offsprings. Another important reason which has been pointed out by a total number of 85 or 57.43 per cent of the respondents appear to be very much justified. They say that, procurement of children is very much essential in human life for fulfilling the ritual requirements specifically in Hindu society. Such ritual requirements are manifold. These are as follows:

*(i)* That both in patrilineal and matrilineal societies, the children, i.e., eldest son in patrilineal and eldest daughter in matrilineal societies are to perform the death rites at the time of death, of parents and performing annual oblation rites for the manes. This is inevitably required for attainment of salvation otherwise the soul remains unsatisfied that may become malevolent and may cause disaster (Case Study-8).

*(ii)* That the children are to perform annual *Sradha* ceremony in order to appease the forefathers or the souls of the dead on the lineal parental line.

*(iii)* That the children may act as social and ritual heads of the family during the absence of parents or when the parents are inactive because of ill health or any other reason.

Two more answers are to be discussed here. Each of these has its own social significance. About 33.78 per cent or 50 aged persons opined that they had procreated children with the hope that they would educate their children, who after receiving education would seek employment and would raise the dignity of their family in the society: 7.43 per cent or 11 aged said that they procreated children with a hope that they would inherit their parental property and maintain the dignity, social prestige or heritage of their family. The rest 21.62 per cent or 32 persons remained neutral and said that they did not have any motive, behind procurement of their children rather they produced them naturally as per the need of the nature.

It was thought appropriate to put a succeeding question on whether the motives behind procurement of children is fulfilled or not. Some respondents answered, whereas some remained indifferent and some did not give any answer. This indicated a conspicuous picture about their dissatisfaction about their children.

A total number of 103 aged persons had nourished a desire for receiving old-age security from their children. Out of them, 45.63 per cent or 47 persons had said that this motive of them has been fully fulfilled and the rest indicated that this hope had been partly fulfilled (16.50%) and 25.24 per cent said that this hope had not been fulfilled (25.24%) and 12.12 per cent did not have any answer. Those who did not give any answer clearly showed their dissatisfaction which was substantiated from their repulsive facial expressions even though they did not utter anything (Table: 5.16). They did not utter their grievances either because of fear or because of emotion.

## Separation of Married Children from the Aged Persons

It is expected from children that they should stay together with their aged parents after their marriage. This provides a special type of gregarious pleasure to the aged as some new members like daughters-in-law and incourse of time, grandchildren join the family. The aged parents-in-law expect some pleasant treatment, like nursing, feeding, comfort etc. from their daughters-in-law, and like to engage themselves with grandchildren. They get much pleasure out of it. But this pious wish of some aged persons is shattered in several ways for various reasons. Some of the important reasons are ill treatment of daughters-in-law or sons for some flimsy reasons. In few cases the married children also get separated from their aged parents because of economic pressure. This is evidenced from the data available in Table 5.17. It indicates that in 11.59 per cent or in 17 cases the children are separated from their aged parents (Case Study 1). But when out of the total of 148 aged persons, 7 respondents or 4.73 per cent of parents and children have been separated, in 6.76 per cent (10) of cases the adopted sons have deserted their parents and lead life separately. This, of course, creates mental tension and leads to loss of mental tranquility of the aged.

## Interaction of the Aged Persons with Sons Staying Outside Home

Socio-economic interaction of the aged with the children who stay outside of parental homes, i.e., at the places of their service or business, is very poor, primarily because of locational disadvantage, that shortens the scope of meeting together frequently. In the present study, in case of 72 or 48.65 per cent of the aged persons, at least one son is serving or doing business and staying away from them (Table 5.18).

Out of the total of 72 aged persons, whose sons (at least one) are staying outside their village, 54 or 75 per cent say that their children often visit them, and the rest 18 or 25 per cent of aged equate the visit of their son/s with 'no-visit' since their visit is very short and infrequent (Table 5.19). However, among those who say that their children visit them, there are only 14 or 26.93 per cent of the aged who say that their children visit them regularly, and as many as 30 persons or 55.56 per cent claim that their children visit them occasionally depending upon their desire or availability of time. The rest 10 persons or 18.52 per cent, however, are not so much satisfied with their outstationed sons as they visit them only during crisis or only when asked (Table 5.20). However, as to the reasons of irregular visit of sons to their aged parents residing it villages, most of the respondents said that it is because of long distance and meagre income of their son/s for which they do not visit regularly their aged parent at village. Next to this reason, a total number of 21 aged persons accounting for 36.21 per cent claim that their sons do not visit them because of their apathy or abhorrence of the wives of their sons towards rural living conditions (Case Study 9).

Another important reason is also there for which the children staying outside do not visit frequently their parents staying in villages. This is because of a strained social relationship which persists between the aged parents and their children due to ideological claim that their children do not neglect them intentionally, rather the proposal of their sons on staying at a place other than the village, is not acceptable to them. They say that their children compel them to stay with them at their working places. But it is not acceptable to the aged parents because of various reasons; the main being the attraction of spending the last part of their life in their native village. Thus, on one hand the aged like to spend their last part of life in their own village where they are born and brought up and on the other hand, their children do not like to reside in villages as villages environment is not conducive for good education for their children, and one has to spend more money on transport for attending office daily. Increasingly, a total number of 13 aged persons accounting for 22.41 per cent have very rightly realised how their children are heavily pressurised in official or in some other day-to-day activities that hinders a regular contact between them, i.e., between aged parents living in village and children working in cities (Table 5.21).

A total number of 5 aged persons (8.62%) remained silent and did not answer to the question. This indicated their displeasure on their children.

When a reverse question relating to the visit of the aged, staying in villages, to their children at cities was asked, about 41.22 per cent or 61 aged persons said that they visit their sons, (Table 5.22) but only 28 or 45.90 per cent of them said that they keep regular contact with their children. On the contrary 18 or 29.51 per cent said that they visit their children only during crisis or when their help is sought. Next to them are 12 persons or 19.67 per cent who said that they visit their children occasionally depending upon their mood and necessity. There are about 5 per cent or 3 aged who said that they visit their children during almost all the festive occasions in which they prepare traditional food items and share those with their sons and grandchildren (Table 5.23) living elsewhere.

Those who do not visit their children have pointed out as many as 7 reasons. Highest percentage (57.50) of the aged say that they are unable to visit their children regularly because of their old age that does not permit strenuous journey. A total number 48 or 40 per cent of aged opined that it is because of the accommodation problem as in most of the cases the rooms are small and hence, not sufficient for all the family members to live comfortably. Another factor which is pointed out by 35 per cent of the aged, is related to the high living-cost in cities, as a result they do not like to pressurise their sons economically by frequently visit in them. And less than 26 per cent say that it is because of their ill health. They are followed by 14.17 per cent of aged who say that they reduce their visit to their sons because of ill treatment of their daughters-in-law and 11.67 per cent say that it is because of the fact that they consume narcotics and smoke which are not tolerated by their sons, and many times their grandchildren oppose it (Table 5.24).

**Financial Assistance of Employed Sons to Aged Parents**

After discussing the problems relating to staying arrangement of the aged, now, it becomes important to analyse the financial assistance they get from their respective sons staying outside the village.

As noted earlier, there are 72 aged persons in which cases at least one of their sons is staying outside village, who is either in salaried service or doing business. But there are only 29 or 40.28 per cent of sons who render financial help to their parents (Table 5.25). About 17.24 per cent or 5 of them regularly remit money every month in order to enable their aged parents for managing their home or for meeting the expenses of some important event, like marriage of a kin, particularly a daughter, a sister or some other kin, annual repairing of house, meeting of medical expenses etc. However, 17 or 58.62 per cent send money as and whenever necessity arises and the rest 7 or 24.14 per cent send it occasionally (Table 5.26). Hence, in most of the cases the aged are to manage themselves with the meagre money they get as their pension or from any other sources. They are to undergo hardships, if they have some unmarried children. In some cases, the employed sons do not render any type of financial help for the marriage of their sisters or brothers and in those cases, the aged remain under psychological stress, which deteriorates their health as some of them suffer from high blood pressure and hypertension, parkinsonism and even heart problems because of this. In this context Case Study 5 may be referred to.

**Involvement of the Aged in Decision-making Process-households and Community Levels**

Decision-making is an important aspect of day-to-day life. Generally, the household head decides everything either solely or in consultation with other family members. However, involvement of persons in decision-making depends on their social status, experience and age. If the social status of a person is subordinate or not honourable or the person is a minor or a very senior, he/she is not involved in the decision-making process either at the household or at the community level. But the role of active aged persons is very crucial because of their experience and deep knowledge in life-management. Still then they are neglected and in many cases their authority is seized and they are not even consulted for their advice.

In this context Table 5.27 indicates that of the total of 67 aged men, merely 25 or 37.31 per cent are heading their family and the rest do not. But comparatively lesser percentage of pensioners (41.82) head their houses than others (16.67). This is because of the fact that the pensioners earn and are more independent than others. This ultimately, recognises their authority in the family and the children do not interfere in it with a fear that the economic contribution of their fathers would be stopped if they go against their parents, particularly pension holding fathers.

As to the reasons of not heading family, highest percentage of aged i.e., 45.24 per cent say that their authority has been seized by their sons and hence they are not honoured. However, 35.71 per cent have voluntarily handed over the responsibility to their sons because of their old age or inability to do the job. But the rest 19.05 per cent are not heading family or not interfering in any familial decision because of their frustration and development of bitterness in their life (Table 5.28). If a cursory look is given on the data available in the said table, an interesting picture comes into the light. When maximum pensioners have handed over their authority to their legitimate sons, there is none among the non-pensioners who has done so. Rather, in 80 per cent of cases, their authority or power has been snatched away by their sons. In this context one may refer to the Case Study 6.

In the above context, we may also discuss the case of the women. It is very obvious that in patriachal societies, the authority of men is quite distinct in various segments of social life. Still then the role of senior women, particularly spouse of the household head is clearly distinct in some sectors, like management of household. She enjoys a superior position in family as compared to other women or daughters in-law. But the situation is changing very fast as the daughters-in-law are not in a position to obey the tradition-bound or the aged women (Case Study 7). They try to diminish the authority of their mothers-in-law in various manners either by imposing of certain restrictions directly or by creating several conflicting situations between their mothers-in-law and husbands. In certain cases they tell lies against their mothers-in-law and try to get the support of their husbands. By the way, the mother-in-law feel frustrated and become subordinate to their daughters-in-law and the clutch of home management comes into the latter's hand. These facts are evidenced from many field realities and these are substantiated statistically in Table 5.29 and 5.30. The former table indicates that there are only 30 or 37.04 per cent of aged women who are now managing their homes in domestic affairs and rest 62.96 per cent do not. As to the reasons, highest percentage of the aged women point out that their authority has been snatched away by their daughters-in-law through various tricky ways. But as many as in 31.37 per cent of cases their sons have actively interfered in compelling their mothers to hand over the authority to their wives. In 11.76 per cent of cases aged women have voluntarily handed over the responsibility of home management to their daughters-in-law because of their old age or inability or in a way to maintain a balanced social relationship between them. The rest are no more managing their homes because of frustration in life (Table 5.30).

**Consultancy with the Aged Persons During Crisis/Difficult Situation**

From the earlier discussions it is perspicacious that the social status of the aged is detrimental. But they are considered as good resources of wisdom, and hence they are consulted during crisis or difficult situations. This is important for the well-being of the family members or society as a whole. Even their simple presence provides moral courage to the younger generation to face such situation bravely. As a result even if a person is very old or physically immobile, he/she is consulted in various matters and in that case they feel happy for their involvement as it gives them satisfaction and pleasure. Still then there are many who are left alone and not consulted or permitted to get involved in difficult situations for renderance of consultancy service. In this context, the present study reveals that there are as many as 53 or 35.81 per cent of aged who are not consulted in any matter concerning to household affairs or during crisis situations at the community levels (Table 5.31).

**Involvement of the Aged Persons in Village Community**

Direct or indirect involvement of the aged in community affairs is very poor since village or community affairs involve various controversies, petty politics and social issues on maintenance of law and order. These cause to increase their psychological trauma, and these also cause deterioration of both physical and mental health of the aged. As a result there are only 13 or 19.40 per cent of aged men who are the official members at community level (Table 5.32). But practically 10 or 14.90 per cent of them directly participate in decision-making at village meetings. The rest attend but do not give any opinion so as to invite any problem for them (Table 5.33). Another aspect of not involving oneself in the process is that in many cases the aged are invited to remain as official members in village communities for the sake of maintaining the tradition, but practically their decisions are not honoured by the younger members. This ultimately hampers the social prestige of the aged. As data provided in Table 5.34, of the total 10 aged who are participants in the community level meetings, only 3 or 30 per cent of them say that in most of the cases their decisions are not accepted. On the other hand, an equal percentage of them opine that in some cases their decision are given due importance. But in case of the rest 40 per cent of the aged, their decision are taken into consideration only in rare cases.

**Family Members Thinking the Aged Persons as Social Burden**

Love, affection and respect are a matter of the state of heart and mind. It is a spontaneous internal impulse which is based on blood tie, nature and bahaviour of a person. In a family, all the members are socially tied with one another because of consanguineal and affinal ties. Socially as well as economically they are all dependent on one another. When a child takes birth, he/she is nourished and brought up under the sustained guidance and maintenance of his/her parents. It is normally hoped that the children should look after their parents when they become old. This social system is unique to the human beings only. But the social value which appears to be there in this system is steadily changing basing on the mobilisation of the traditional social systems and values. In the changing scenario, many individuals of the younger generation have become materialistic and individualistic and are forgetting their duty towards their senior family members, particularly the aged parents. Even many consider them as social burden and hence want that they should die as soon as possible so that they would get relieved from nursing duties (Case Study 1, 2, 3 etc.) or from economic pressure. In this context, we may refer to the data presented in Table 5.35. It is observed that in respect of 3 or 2.03 per cent of the aged, their own sons consider them as social burden. But a total number of 24 or 16.21 per cent of the aged experience that their daughters-in-law are considering them as burden. There are as many as 52 or 35.14 per cent of aged who did not answer. This, of course indicate that they are considered as such by some of their family members, particularly by their sons or daughters-in-law. The rest 68 or 45.95 per cent of aged however, opine that nobody in their family considers them as burden.

### Food and Narcotic Habits Among the Aged

Food is the basic requirement for sustenance of life. Without it no one can think of life. Hence, it is very essential for all irrespective of age and sex. But one has to give more importance on the diet of the aged persons. Because an imbalanced diet may hasten up deterioration of their health causing malnutrition, and diseases and even sudden death.

A balanced diet required for the Indian aged (above 60 years) has been recommended by National Institute of Nutrition, Hyderabad. It constitutes various cereals, vegetables, fruits, fats and oils with approximate nutrients supplied by these foodstuff (Appendix 7). But generally there are very few conscious aged who are serious about consumption of a balanced diet. Similarly there are also very few children who are very conscious to provide to it their aged parents. This might be due to their poverty or because of some other factors. However, during old age, many aged become very choosy about their food and some others take to over-consumption. This results in various problems.

### Food Habit and the Aged

Remaining vegetarian or non-vegetarian is a matter of socio-religious factor. It also depends upon ones own choice. In the present study more aged women (29.63%) than men (5.97%) are vegetarian (Table 5.36) as in orthodox caste Hindu societies, abstaining from non-vegetarian diet by the aged women, particularly widows, is purely a cultural factor. They are to follow it with a view to respecting the soul of the deceased husbands and earning ritual merits thereby. This, of course, compels them to lead an austere life style. In many cases, they cannot breakup the tradition even if they desire to consume non-vegetarian foodstuff. However, even though 94.09 per cent of aged men as against 70.37 per cent of aged women are non-vegetarian, altogether only about 29 per cent of them point out fish (14.191), meat/chicken (10.81%) or egg (4.05%) to be their most favourite food items. But the most important food item which is liked by most of them (30%) is milk. Sweet is the most wanted occasional item for about 9 per cent of the aged. Interestingly less then 7 per cent say that they like sweet mango as the most important fruit partly because it is tasty and partly because it is easily eatable by the aged who have lost their teeth. A total number of 4 aged persons accounting for 2.70 per cent grade cheese as their most favourite food (Table 5.37). But practically all of them do not get their favourite foodstuff as per their desire. When there are only 5.16 per cent or 6 aged persons who get their favourite foodstuff whenever they want, there are as many as 35.34 per cent or 41 of them who are provided with their favourite foodstuff in rare cases. In-between these two groups of aged, 12.07 per cent say that they get their favourite food items most frequently. They are followed by an equal percentage of aged persons who opine that they get such foodstuff frequently (Table 5.38).

So far as the daily food is concerned, 31.08 per cent or 46 are fully satisfied with the food they are provided with. Nearly about 49 per cent or 72 of them are partially satisfied and the rest 20.27 per cent or 30 aged are not at all satisfied (Table 5.39). Thus, if the aged who are "partially satisfied" and "not satisfied" categories are added together, they constitute a large chunck who remain unsatisfied with their daily food. This happens as because, in many cases the aged are given second preference. (Case Study 15).

## Narcotic Habit and Alcoholism among the Aged

Aged people are normally addicted to various narcotics. The frequency of consumption of narcotics increases during this age as it helps them to adjust with leisure time. They also consume it when they do not have any work to do. These factors have made a total number of 110 or 74.32 per cent of aged addicted to different narcotics and alcohol (Table 5.40).

There are more aged men (77.61%) than aged women (71.60%) who are addicted. Men are addicted to as many as 6 items such as *bidi* (42.31%), *tamakhu* or tobacco paste (38.46%), betel (34.62%), ganja (7.69%), *Khaini* (7.69%), and alcohol (3.85%). But aged women are addicted to only 3 items such as betel (65.52%), *Tamakhu* (48.28%), and *Khaini* (1.72%). Thus, when most of the aged men are addicted to *bidi*, it is betel for the aged women (Table 5.41).

## Health, Disease and the Process of Treatment

Becoming old is a bio-physiological process by which the aged gradually lose strength because of weakening of muscular and cardio-vascular systems. Coinciding with the advancement of age and weakening of these systems, some specific diseases occur among the aged. So, almost all the aged suffer from at least one because of their senility and debility.

## Physical Mobility and the Aged

When a person loses his/her vigour and physical strength because of age, he/she becomes unable to move. However, he/she may move with the help of a person or a walking-stick. In this respect Table 5.42 reveals that maximum, i.e., 89 or 60.14 per cent of the aged are quite mobile without the help of anybody but a total number of 29 or 19.59 per cent are fairly mobile. However, they do not take the help of walking-sticks. They are followed by 19 or 12.84 per cent of aged who are fairly mobile with the help of walking-sticks. A total number of 6 or 4.05 per cent are slightly mobile. But certainly they move with the help of others. The rest 5 or 3.38 per cent are found to be bedridden and hence completely immobile.

**Aged Persons Suffering from at least One Disease**

The aged who suffer from at-least one disease constitute 130 persons or 87.84 per cent of the total sample of 148 (Table 5.43). But the most important disease from which the highest percentage, i.e., 20.77 of aged irrespective of sex suffer from, is rheumatism or joint pain. However, the diseases from which the aged men suffer are rheumatism (18 or 29.03%), constipation (15 or 24.19%), high blood pressure (14 or 22.58%), weak eye sight (14 or 22.58%), asthma (11 of 17.74%), diabetes (9 or 14.51%), cough and cold (7 or 11.29%), gastric (7 or 11.29%), giddiness (7 or 11.29%), heart problem (6 or 9.68%), forgetfulness (5 or 8.06%), filaria (3 or 4.84%), hearing problem (3 or 4.84%), piles (3 or 4.84%), urinary problem (3 or 4.84%), low blood pressure (2 or 3.22%), partial paralysis (2 or 3.28%) and parkinsionism (1 or 1.61%).

The most important disease from which highest percentage of the aged women suffer is found to be weak eye sight (12 or 17.65%). They are followed by those who suffer from high blood pressure (11 or 16.18%), rheumatism (9 or 13.24%), asthma (8 or 11.76%), constipation (8 or 11.76%), cold and cough (6 or 8.82%), giddiness (6 or 8.82%), heart problem (4 or 5.88%), piles (4 or 5.88%), forgetfulness (7 or 4.41%), hearing problem (3 or 4.41%), waist/back pain (3 or 4.41%), colic/peptic ulcer (2 or 2.94%), diabetes (2 or 2.94%), partial loss of speech (2 or 2.94%), low blood pressure (1 or 1.47%), filaria (1 or 1.47%), partial paralysis (1 or 1.47%) and the rest 1 or 1.47 per cent suffers from urinary problem.

The total figures represent that maximum aged irrespective of sex suffer from rheumatism (27 or 20.77%) and at least 10 per cent of them suffer from weak eye sight (26 or 20.00%), high blood pressure (25 or 19.23%) constipation (23 or 17.69%), asthma (19 or 14.62%), cold and cough (13 or 10%), and giddiness (13 or 10%). The other diseases from which the aged suffer constitute less than 10 per cent against each disease (Table: 5.44).

From the total of 130 aged persons who are suffering from at least one disease, only 28 or 21.54 per cent are undergoing treatment. But more aged men (30.65%) than aged women

(13.24%) are being treated for their diseases (Table 5.45). This is because, in traditional societies, the women are neglected more than men in various ways. Normally, due importance is not given on the health aspect of the women. This happens because the men are considered as the superior sex compared to that of women in patriarchal societies and in that case women generally opt for utilising the scarce monetary resource on the treatment of diseases of their husbands. On the other hand, the men who earn money, do not attach much importance to the health of women unless they are very serious. A further look at the same table points out that comparatively more pensioners undergo treatment for the diseases they are suffering from. This is because, they earn, move outside without any social restriction and at the same time they are very conscious about their own health.

So far as the type of treatment is concerned, highest percentage (71.43) of aged use allopathic medicine followed by 17.86 per cent who are undergoing homoeopathic treatment. Thus, there is a big gap between the persons using alloeopathic medicine and those who use homoeopathic and ayurvedic medicine (Table 5.46).

However, in most of the cases (64.29%) the aged themselves bear the cost of medicine. In 14.29 per cent of cases, the cost is met by both the aged and their sons but 10.71 per cent say that the cost is exclusively met by their sons. As the housewives are non-earning numbers, the cost of their treatment is either met by their husbands or sons or both of them (Table: 5.47). But even if majority of the aged bear the cost of the medicine required for their treatment, it is found that only 32.14 per cent are fully satisfied with the treatment they are undergoing. This is because, even though they earn and bear the cost of their own treatment, in most of the cases they are to share their income with their whole family members. As a result of this, they are to reduce their budget on personal health. The aged persons who are partially satisfied account for 35.71 per cent and the rest are not at all satisfied with the treatment they are undergoing (Table 5.48).

**Leisure and Recreational Activities Among the Aged Persons**

Leisure is that part of one's daily life in which a person finds himself/herself free from his/her daily callings and engages himself/herself in any work that gives him/her pleasure.

In the dictionary of sociology leisure is defined as "the time free from work and routine domestic responsibilities and available for use in recuperation, relaxation, hobbies, recreational and cultural and artistic pursuits", (1995-364).

According to the international dictionary of English, leisure is "the time when you are not working or doing other duties" (1996: 810).

Depending upon one's age and age-based daily activities, use off leisure is categorised into 4 broad sections, viz., (i) leisure of the working class, (ii) leisure of the unemployed, (iii) leisure of the leisure class and (iv) leisure of the retired persons or the aged.

As age advances or when a person becomes aged or is retired from his/her active life, he/she gets more free time. Most of them feel lonely as circumstances compel them to lead life alone. But comparatively more retired officials/pensioners (67.27%) feel lonely than the non-pensioners (32.73%). This is because the government/non-government officials normally lead a routine life during their service period and they are almost habituated to it. They spend their time from 10 A.M to 5 PM daily in official work and hence they have an opportunity to come in contact with many and various types of people. Retirement and complete detachment from official work causes mental depression in them.

They cannot easily adjust with the demanding situations. They try to keep themselves away from the society either because of their egocentric social prestige or because of some other reasons, like keeping oneself away from village petty politics or other such issues. This is why maximum percentage of pensioners feel highly isolated or lonely after their retirement (Table: 5.49 and 5.50).

An aged person feels very lonely when he/she loses his/her life partner or any of his contemporary friends. Table 5.51 reveals that out of the total 8 number of 148 aged persons, 28 or 18.42 per cent do not have any friend with whom they can share their happiness and griefs. The rest, however, have at least one friend with whom they have intimacy and hence they share their personal feelings on their daily life or on some other topics.

Playing cards and reading of sacred books or listening to the religious recitation like *Ramayana, Bhagbat Gita* are the two important ways of spending time among the aged in traditional Indian villages. Normally card is played during day time among the aged contemporaries of either sexes but religious scripts are recited in evening, preferably at the premises of *Bhagabat-Ghar* or on the front *verandah* of the reader or at a place which is convenient for maximum number of aged to listen the recitation. It gives pleasure to both the readers and the listeners and both earn ritual merits by doing this.

Reading or reciting of religious scripts depends on once education and artistic skills of presentation. So, normally, many read it, silently at home for self-satisfaction and thereby earn ritual gains, but few present it loudly in public depending upon their skill and ability of presentation and interest.

It is evident from the Table 5.52 that 31.34 per cent of aged men as against about 15 per cent of women either read religious scripts or listen to the recitation regularly. But about 25 per cent of men as against 11 per cent of women read or listen to it occasionally. Altogether there are about 40 per cent of aged who, either read religious scripts or listen to the recitation.

Playing cards and *Pasa* are two games which are played by the aged but while the former game is played by both men and women, the latter one is specific to men only. As a result when 37.16 per cent of aged belonging to either sexes play cards, there are only 3.38 per cent of men who play *pasa*. However, so far as playing of cards is concerned, when as many as 38 or 56.72 per cent of men play it, there are only 17 or 20.99 per cent of women who engage themselves in this game and get pleasure out of it.

Gossiping or spending leisure hour at the village tea stalls or community pandals is one of the important leisure time activity. People gather at these places and exchange their feelings with one another at evening hour. But the women are never a part of it, since the society does not permit them to do so. However, there are 47 or 31.76 per cent aged men who spend time in it and get relaxed.

Due to the technological advancement, now-a-days, television has reached to maximum persons and it has been one of the most important media of entertainment as it provides both picture and sound. But in rural sectors television is not found in all the households because of poverty. However, there are 14 or 20 per cent of men as against 7 or 8.64 per cent of women who regularly watch it. If the persons who occasionally watch T.V. are added with the number of regular viewers, the total aged men comes to be 21 or 31.34 per cent as against 14 or 17.28 per cent of women.

Those who listen to radio regularly or occasionally constitute 19 or 28.36 per cent of men and 7 or 8.64 per cent of women. But more men are habituated to listening of news, programmes on agriculture etc., the women mainly listen to songs which may be patriotic, devotional or similar ones.

Reading of newspaper is found to be a habit of men only. This might be because of their education and wider world view than the women who are normally illiterate and confined to home only. However, there is only one women who says that she goes through some story books occasionally depending upon the availability of such books. On the contrary the men who regularly read story books account for 10 or 14.93 per cent as against 7 or 10.45 per cent who read such books occasionally. There are 16 or 23.88 per cent of aged men as against 9 or 11.11 per cent of women who simply sit at home.

**Old Age and Drawal of Pension**

Government provides various benefits to its servants during their lifetime. After retirement from government service, the employees are entitled to get monthly pension for their subsistence. This has been ensured with a view to protecting the basic interests of the government servants. But, the procedure of drawal of pension involves many problems which must be taken care of by the state government. Steps must be taken to reduce the unnecessary inconveniences involved in it.

Presently there are two ways of getting pension. One way to get it is from the state treasuries and the other way is to draw from the lead banks.

**Existing Treasuries and Drawal of Pension**

In the district of Khurdha there is one district treasury located in Bhubaneswar city. Under this treasury, there are 4 sub-treasuries; and of these 4 sub-treasuries, one is located in Khurdha, one in Jatni, one in Tangi and the rest one in Banpur. Apart from these, there is another treasury called 'special treasury' which is located within the Bhubaneswar city, i.e., Bapujee Nagar. This treasury has been established with the prime objective of reducing the workload of the district treasury, Khurdha. However, the retired persons who reside in and around Bhubaneswar city mainly depend on these two treasuries, viz, the district treasury, Khurdha, and the special treasury, Bhubaneswar, for drawal of their pension and other dues from the government account. But practically, it is very difficult and painstaking task for the aged pensioners, particularly those who reside in rural areas, to come over to Bhuabaneswar and draw their pension from treasuries because of the following reasons:

*(i)* The aged retired employees are to come over to Bhubaneswar city personally even against their ill health in order to justify their existence.

*(ii)* They are to climb up to the first floor since the treasuries are not located on the ground floor.

*(iii)* The number of pensioners in quite high (Appendix 8). This makes a crowd within the premises of treasuries. So, they are to stand in long queues for a long time.

*(iv)* There is no sitting arrangement for the pensioners in the premises of the treasuries. It results in fatigue, and weariness.

(*v*) Arrears are disbursed only after 10th day of every month. So, an aged person has to come over to the city twice if he/she has some dues to get as arrear.

On the contrary, the officials of the treasuries experience a lot of inconveniences. Even though, different dates have been earmarked for drawal of pension of different category of pensioners (Appendix 9), most of them do not bother about it and come on the 1st working day of every month and in that case, the officials are indirectly compelled to look after all of them out of humanitarian ground. Otherwise, many helpless aged pensioners are to return home and come again to Bhubaneswar.

As shown in Appendix 7 more number of pensioners (62.26%), irrespective of any category, draw their pension from treasuries than those who have opted to get it from public sector lead banks (37.74%). Similarly, the present study shows that quite a high percentage of pensioners (78.18) and family-pension holders (80.95) draw pension from the treasuries instead of getting in from public sector lead banks (Table 5.53).

**Existing Public Sector Lead Banks and Drawal of Pension**

The lead banks through which pension transactions are made, are eight. These are:

1. State Bank of India,
2. United Commercial Bank,
3. Bank of India,
4. Indian Bank,
5. Commercial Bank,
6. United Bank of India,
7. Indian Overseas Bank, and
8. Central Bank.

For the pensioners, it is easy and less painstaking to draw pension from any one of the above lead banks since a pensioner or family-pension holder can drawn his/her pension on any working day depending upon the requirement and suitability. But many people do not get the facility either because of their low awareness or because of the fact that it involves a difficult task to process the application form for getting pension from any one lead bank. Another factor for which the retired persons do not opt to draw their pension from the lead banks, is that they experience a delayed procedure to get their arrears from such banks which does not happen so in treasuries.

**Table—5.1: Family types among the aged**

| *Family type* | *Total cases* | *% age* |
|---|---|---|
| Nuclear | 49 | 33.11 |
| Sub-nuclear | 2 | 1.35 |
| Vertically extended | 69 | 46.62 |
| Supplemented | 27 | 18.24 |
| Broken | 1 | 0.68 |
| **Total** | **148** | **100.00** |

**Table—5.2: Number of generations staying together**

| *No. of generations* | *Total cases* | *% age* |
|---|---|---|
| 1 | 17 | 11.49 |
| 2 | 43 | 29.05 |
| 3 | 88 | 59.46 |
| **Total** | **148** | **100.00** |

**Table—5.3: Ascending and descending generations living with the aged**

| *Generations* | *Total cases* | *% age* |
|---|---|---|
| Ego without its own generation | 26 | 17.57 |
| Ego with its own generation | 122 | 82.43 |
| Ego with its 1st ascending generation | 2 | 1.35 |
| Ego with its 1st descending generation | 129 | 87.16 |
| Ego with its 2nd descending generation | 87 | 58.78 |

**Table—5.4: Kins living with the aged**

| Sl. No. | Family members | Category of aged | | | | | | | Total |
|---|---|---|---|---|---|---|---|---|---|
| | | Pensioners | Family pension pension | Housewives | Retired from private sectors | Old farmers | Old business men | Old wage earners | |
| (1) | (2) | (3) | (4) | (5) | (6) | (7) | (8) | (9) | (10) |
| 1. | Living only with spouses | 5 (9.09) | – | 8 (13.33) | – | 2 (66.67) | 1 (33.33) | 1 (33.33) | 17 (11.49) |
| 2. | Living with spouse and unmarried children | 16 (29.09) | – | 16 (26.67) | – | – | – | – | 32 (21.62) |
| 3. | Living with spouse and married children but without having grandchildren | 3 (5.45) | – | 3 (5.00) | – | – | – | – | 6 (4.05) |
| 4. | Living with spouse, married children and unmarried grand-children | 23 (41.82) | – | 27 (45.0) | 2 (66.67) | 1 (33.33) | 1 (33.33) | 2 (66.67) | 56 (37.84) |
| 5. | Living with spouse, married and unmarried children and unmarried grandchildren | 2 (3.64) | – | 3 (5.00) | – | – | – | – | 5 (3.38) |
| 6. | Living with spouse and married children of daughter | 1 (1.82) | – | – | – | – | – | – | 1 (0.68) |

(Contd...)

| (1) | (2) | (3) | (4) | (5) | (6) | (7) | (8) | (9) | (10) |
|---|---|---|---|---|---|---|---|---|---|
| 7. | Living with spouse and grandchildren | 1 (1.82) | – | 1 (1.67) | – | – | – | – | 2 (1.35) |
| 8. | Living with spouse father and unmarried children | 1 (1.82) | – | 1 (1.67) | – | – | – | – | 2 (1.35) |
| 9. | Living with spouse, unmarried children, daughter's children and wife's sister | 1 (1.82) | – | 1 (1.67) | – | – | – | – | 2 (1.35) |
| 10. | Living along (without spouse) with unmarried children | 1 (1.82) | 1 (4.76) | – | – | – | – | – | 2 (1.35) |
| 11. | Living alone (without spouse) with son's wife and grandchildren | – | 1 (4.76) | – | – | – | – | – | 1 (0.68) |
| 12. | Living alone (without spouse) with married son and grandchildren | 1 (1.82) | 18 (85.71) | – | 1 (33.33) | – | 1 (33.33) | – | 21 (14.19) |
| 13. | Living alone (without spouse) with married and unmarried children and grandchildren | – | 1 (4.76) | – | – | – | – | – | 1 (0.68) |
| | **Total** | **55 (100.00)** | **21 (100.00)** | **60 (100.00)** | **3 (100.00)** | **3 (100.00)** | **3 (100.00)** | **3 (100.00)** | **148 (100.00)** |

*Note:* Figures in brackets represent % age.

**Table—5.5: Availability of living-rooms**

| *No. of rooms* | *Persons posess* | *% age* |
|---|---|---|
| Nil | 1 | 0.68 |
| 1 | 17 | 11.49 |
| 2 | 63 | 42.57 |
| 3 | 48 | 32.43 |
| 4 | 15 | 10.14 |
| 5 | 5 | 3.38 |
| **Total** | **148** | **100.00** |

**Table—5.6: Whether the available living-rooms are sufficient for all the family members?**

| *Answers* | *Male* | *Female* | *Total* |
|---|---|---|---|
| Yes | 37<br>(55.22) | 22<br>(27.16) | 59<br>(39.86) |
| No | 30<br>(44.78) | 59<br>(72.84) | 89<br>(60.14) |
| **Total** | **67<br>(100.00)** | **81<br>(100.00)** | **148<br>(100.00)** |

*Note:* Figures in brackets represent % age.

**Table—5.7: Whether you have a separate living room?**

| | *Frequency* | | | *Have* | | | *Don't have* | | |
|---|---|---|---|---|---|---|---|---|---|
| *Category of* | *M* | *F* | *T* | *M* | *F* | *T* | *M* | *F* | *T* |
| Persons having 'yes' answers | 37<br>(100.00) | 22<br>(100.00) | 59<br>(100.00) | 13<br>(35.14) | 7<br>(31.82) | 20<br>(33.90) | 24<br>(64.86) | 15<br>(68.18) | 39<br>(66.10) |
| Persons having 'No' answers | 30<br>(100.00) | 59<br>(100.00) | 89<br>(100.00) | 3<br>(10.00) | 10<br>(16.95) | 13<br>(14.61) | 27<br>(90.00) | 49<br>(83.05) | 76<br>(85.39) |
| **Total** | **67**<br>**(100.00)** | **81**<br>**(100.00)** | **148**<br>**(100.00)** | **16**<br>**(23.88)** | **13**<br>**(16.05)** | **29**<br>**(19.59)** | **51**<br>**(76.12)** | **68**<br>**(83.95)** | **119**<br>**(80.41)** |

*Note*: Figures in brackets represent % age.

**Table—5.8: Place of staying among aged who do not have separate living rooms**

| *Places* | *Men (N = 51)* | *Women (N = 68)* | *Total (N = 119)* |
|---|---|---|---|
| Enclosed verandah of own house | 18 (35.29) | 8 (11.76) | 26 (21.85) |
| Enclosed verandah of neighbour's house | 1 (1.96) | - | 1 (0.84) |
| Etrance-room | 22 (43.14) | 13 (19.12) | 35 (29.41) |
| Adjusted in any room/place | 7 (13.73) | 47 (69.12) | 54 (45.38) |
| *Bhagabat Ghar* | 1 (1.96) | - | 1 (0.84) |
| Abandoned cowshed | 2 (3.92) | - | 2 (1.68) |

*Note:* Figures in brackets represent % age.

**Table—5.9: Income of the aged (pensioner's and family-pension holders)**

| *Income range (In Rs.)* | *Frequency* | | *Total* |
|---|---|---|---|
| | *Pensioners* | *Family pension holders* | |
| <1000 | 2 (3.64) | 1 (4.76) | 3 (3.95) |
| 1000-1500 | 30 (54.55) | 15 (71.43) | 45 (59.21) |
| 1500-2000 | 10 (18.18) | 5 (23.81) | 15 (19.74) |
| 2001-2500 | 7 (12.73) | - | 7 (9.21) |
| 2501-3000 | 2 (3.64) | - | 2 (2.64) |
| 3001 and above | 4 (7.27) | - | 4 (5.26) |
| **Total** | **55 (100.00)** | **21 (100.00)** | **76 (100.00)** |

*Note:* Figures in brackets represent % age.

**Table—5.10: Average income earned among aged (pensioners and family-pension holders)**

| *Income Range (in Rs.)* | *Total pensioners* | *Total income earned* | *Av. per person* | *Total FPHs* | *Total income earned* | *Av. per person* | *Both pensioners and FPHs* | *Grand total* | |
|---|---|---|---|---|---|---|---|---|---|
| | | | | | | | | *Total income earned* | *Av. per person* |
| <1000 | 2 | 1892 | 946.00 | 1 | 800 | 800.00 | 3 | 2692 | 897.33 |
| 1001-1500 | 30 | 37140 | 1238.00 | 15 | 19238 | 1282.53 | 45 | 56378 | 1252.84 |
| 1501-2000 | 10 | 17332 | 1733.00 | 5 | 9142 | 1828.40 | 15 | 26474 | 1764.93 |
| 2001-2500 | 7 | 15618 | 2231.14 | – | – | – | 7 | 15618 | 2231.14 |
| 2501-3000 | 2 | 15618 | 2807.50 | – | – | – | 2 | 15618 | 2807.50 |
| 3001 and above | 4 | 13805 | 3451.25 | – | – | – | 4 | 13805 | 3451.25 |
| **Total** | **55** | **101405** | **1843.73** | **21** | **29180** | **1389.52** | **76** | **130585** | **1718.22** |

**Table—5.11: Expenditure pattern of the aged (pensioners and FPHs)**

| *Variables* | *Pensioners* | *Family pension holders* | *Total* |
|---|---|---|---|
| Keep the whole income (pension) with self and manage the home | 28 (50.91) | 3 (14.29) | 31 (40.79) |
| Partly keep with self and partly give to son for home management | 15 (27.27) | 2 (9.52) | 17 (22.37) |
| Give the whole income (pension) to son for home management | 12 (21.82) | 16 (76.19) | 28 (36.84) |
| **Total** | **55(100.00)** | **21(100.00)** | **76(100.00)** |

*Note:* Figures in brackets represent % age.

**Table—5.12: Participation of Non-bedridden aged men and women in daily life**

| Sl. No. | Activities | Male | | | Female | | | Total | | |
|---|---|---|---|---|---|---|---|---|---|---|
| | | F | O | T | F | O | T | F | O | T |
| 1. | Supervision of agricultural work | 21 (32.81) | 26 (40.63) | 47 (73.43) | 8 (10.13) | 8 (10.13) | 16 (20.25) | 29 (20.28) | 34 (23.78) | 63 (44.06) |
| 2. | Looking after domestic animals | 22 (34.38) | 11 (17.19) | 33 (51.56) | 6 (7.59) | 13 (16.56) | 19 (24.05) | 28 (19.58) | 24 (16.78) | 52 (36.36) |
| 3. | Shopping | 18 (28.13) | 25 (39.06) | 43 (67.19) | 7 (8.86) | 18 (22.78) | 25 (31.65) | 25 (17.48) | 43 (30.07) | 68 (47.55) |
| 4. | Cooking | 1 (1.56) | 7 (10.94) | 8 (12.50) | 18 (22.78) | 12 (15.19) | 30 (37.97) | 19 (13.29) | 19 (13.29) | 38 (26.57) |
| 5. | Cleaning utencils /house floor | 1 (1.56) | 7 (10.94) | 8 (12.50) | 30 (37.97) | 23 (29.11) | 53 (67.09) | 31 (21.68) | 30 (20.98) | 61 (42.66) |
| 6. | Washing clothes | 1 (1.56) | 4 (6.25) | 5 (7.81) | 5 (6.33) | 7 (8.86) | 12 (15.19) | 6 (4.20) | 11 (7.69) | 17 (11.89) |
| 7. | Baby sitter | – | 2 (3.13) | 2 (3.13) | 13 (16.46) | 21 (26.58) | 34 (43.04) | 13 (9.09) | 23 (16.08) | 36 (25.17) |
| 8. | Looking after the education of grandchildren | 17 (26.56) | 7 (10.94) | 24 (37.50) | 7 (8.86) | 3 (3.80) | 10 (12.66) | 24 (16.78) | 10 (6.99) | 34 (23.78) |
| 9. | Attending relatives | 20 (31.25) | 13 (20.31) | 33 (51.56) | 3 (3.80) | 17 (21.52) | 20 (25.32) | 23 (16.08) | 30 (20.98) | 54 (37.76) |

*Note:* (i) F = Frequently, O = Occasionally and T = Total

(ii) Figures in brackets represent % age.

**Table—5.13: Work pressure on the aged**

| *Sl. No.* | *Activities* | *N* | *Out of own interest* | *Out of compulsion* | *Out of the situation* |
|---|---|---|---|---|---|
| 1. | Supervision of agricultural work | 63 (100.00) | 27 (42.86) | 16 (25.40) | 20 (31.75) |
| 2. | Looking after domestic animals | 52 (100.00) | 30 (57.69) | 4 (7.69) | 18 (34.62) |
| 3. | Shopping | 68 (100.00) | 18 (26.47) | 12 (17.65) | 38 (55.88) |
| 4. | Cooking | 38 (100.00) | 12 (31.58) | 18 (47.36) | 8 (21.05) |
| 5. | Cleaning utensils/house floor | 61 (100.00) | 37 (60.66) | 20 (32.79) | 4 (6.56) |
| 6. | Cleaning clothes | 17 (100.00) | 3 (17.65) | 7 (41.18) | 7 (41.18) |
| 7. | Baby sitter | 36 (100.00) | 26 (72.22) | 3 (8.33) | 7 (19.44) |
| 8. | Looking after the education of grandchildren | 34 (100.00) | 23 (67.65) | – | 11 (32.35) |
| 9. | Attending relatives | 54 (100.00) | 28 (51.85) | 13 (24.07) | 13 (24.07) |

*Note:* Figures in brackets represent % age.

**Table—5.14: Consequences if the aged do not work**

| *Consequences* | *Aged men (N = 64)* | *Aged women (N = 79)* | *Total (N = 143)* |
|---|---|---|---|
| Son irritates | 22 (34.38) | 3 (3.80) | 25 (17.48) |
| Dauguter-in-law irritates | 5 (7.81) | 27 (34.18) | 32 (22.38) |
| No reaction from any family member | 37 (57.81) | 49 (62.03) | 86 (60.14) |

*Note:* Figures in brackets represent % age.

**Table—5.15: Motives behind procreating children**

| *Sl. No.* | *Motives* | *Male aged (N = 67)* | *Female aged (N = 81)* | *Total (N = 148)* |
|---|---|---|---|---|
| 1. | Old-age security | 37 (55.22) | 66 (81.48) | 103 (69.59) |
| 2. | Fulfilling the ritual requirement | 42 (62.69) | 43 (53.09) | 85 (57.43) |
| 3. | To make them educated and employed | 37 (55.22) | 13 (16.65) | 50 (33.78) |
| 4. | To make them able to sustain the dignity of family | 8 (11.94) | 3 (3.70) | 11 (7.43) |
| 5. | To attain parenthood | 44 (65.67) | 72 (88.89) | 116 (78.38) |
| 6. | Do not have any motive | 23 (34.33) | 9 (11.11) | 32 (21.62) |

*Note:* Figures in brackets represent % age.

**Table—5.16: Fulfilment of motives behind procreation of children**

| *Sl. No.* | *Motives* | *N* | *Fully fulfilled* | *Partly fulfilled* | *Not fulfilled* | *No answer* |
|---|---|---|---|---|---|---|
| 1. | Old-age security | 103<br>(100.00) | 47<br>(45.63) | 17<br>(16.50) | 26<br>(25.24) | 13<br>(12.62) |
| 2. | To make them educated and employed | 50<br>(100.00) | 6<br>(12.00) | 18<br>(36.00) | 26<br>(52.00) | – |
| 3. | To make them able to retain the dignity and social prestige of family | 11<br>(100.00) | 2<br>(18.18) | 2<br>(18.18) | 7<br>(63.64) | –<br>– |
| 4. | To attain parenthood | 116<br>(100.00) | 113<br>(97.41) | –<br>– | 3<br>(2.59) | – |

*Note:* Figures in brackets represent % age.

**Table—5.17: Separation of married sons from aged parents**

| *Category of aged* | *Total sample* | *Separated Own* | *Children adopted* | *Total* |
|---|---|---|---|---|
| Pensioners | 55<br>(100.00) | 3<br>(5.45) | 1<br>(1.82) | 4<br>(7.27) |
| Family-pension holders | 21<br>(100.00) | – | – | – |
| Housewives | 60<br>(100.00) | 3<br>(5.00) | 4<br>(6.67) | 7<br>(11.67) |
| Retired from private sector jobs | 3<br>(100.00) | – | 1<br>(33.33) | 1<br>(33.33) |
| Old farmers | 3<br>(100.00) | 1<br>(33.33) | – | 1<br>(33.33) |
| Old business men | 3<br>(100.00) | – | 2<br>(66.67) | 2<br>(66.67) |
| Old wage-earner | 3<br>(100.00) | – | 2<br>(66.67) | 2<br>(66.67) |
| **Total** | **148**<br>**(100.00)** | **7**<br>**(4.73)** | **10**<br>**(6.76)** | **17**<br>**(11.59)** |

*Note:* Figures in brackets represent % age.

**Table—5.18: No. of cases in which at least one son of the aged serving or doing business and staying away from aged parents**

| *Category of aged* | *Total sample* | *Total cases* | *% age* |
|---|---|---|---|
| Men | 67 | 36 | 53.73 |
| Women | 81 | 36 | 44.44 |
| **Total** | **148** | **72** | **48.65** |

**Table—5.19: Do the employed sons staying outside visit you? (N = 72)**

| *Answers* | *Total cases* | *% age* |
|---|---|---|
| Yes | 54 | 75.00 |
| No | 18 | 25.00 |

**Table—5.20: Frequency of visits of sons staying outside village**

| *Frequency* | *Total cases* | *% age* |
|---|---|---|
| Regularly | 14 | 26.93 |
| Occasionaily depending upon their mood or availability at time | 30 | 55.56 |
| Only when asked/during crisis | 10 | 18.52 |
| **Total** | **54** | **100.00** |

**Table—5.21: Reasons of not visiting parents at all or regularly among sons staying outside (N = 58)**

| *Sl. No.* | *Reasons* | *Total cases* | *% age* |
|---|---|---|---|
| 1. | Long distance/small salary of son | 28 | 48.27 |
| 2. | Dislikeness of daughter-in-law to rural area | 21 | 36.21 |
| 3. | Heavy official pressure/no time | 13 | 22.41 |
| 4. | As we do not stay with them | 18 | 31.03 |
| 5. | Bitter relationship | 12 | 20.69 |
| 6. | No answer | 5 | 8.62 |

**Table—5.22: Do you visit your son staying outside village?**

| *Answer* | *Total cases* | *% age* |
|---|---|---|
| Yes | 61 | 41.22 |
| No | 87 | 58.78 |
| **Total** | **148** | **100.00** |

**Table—5.23: Frequency of visits of aged to their children staying outside (N = 61)**

| *Frequency* | *Total cases* | *% age* |
|---|---|---|
| Regularly | 28 | 45.90 |
| Occasionally/depending upon the mood | 12 | 19.67 |
| On all/most of the festive occasions | 3 | 4.92 |
| When asked/during crisis/requirement | 18 | 29.51 |

**Table—5.24: Reasons of not visiting sons at all or regularly among aged parents (N = 120)**

| *Reasons* | *Total cases* | *% age* |
|---|---|---|
| Ill health | 31 | 25.83 |
| Old age/strenuous journey/long distance | 69 | 57.50 |
| Small room | 48 | 40.00 |
| Do not like to be burden on sons at city | 42 | 35.00 |
| Ill treatment of son | 6 | 5.00 |
| Ill treatment of daughter-in-law | 17 | 14.17 |
| Problem for consumption of narcotics | 14 | 11.67 |

**Table—5.25: Do the sons staying outside remit money (N = 72)**

| *Answers* | *Total cases* | *% age* |
|---|---|---|
| Yes | 29 | 40.28 |
| No | 43 | 59.72 |

**Table—5.26: Frequency of sending money to aged parents staying at village (N = 29)**

| *Frequency* | *Total cases* | *% age* |
|---|---|---|
| Regularly | 5 | 17.24 |
| Occasionally | 7 | 24.14 |
| As and when asked | 17 | 58.62 |

**Table—5.27: No. of aged men heading family**

| *Category* | *Heading* | *Not heading* | *Total* |
|---|---|---|---|
| Pensioners | 23<br>(41.82) | 32<br>(58.18) | 55<br>(100.00) |
| Others | 2<br>(16.67) | 10<br>(83.33) | 12<br>(100.00) |
| **Total** | **25**<br>**(37.31)** | **42**<br>**(62.69)** | **67**<br>**(100.00)** |

*Note:* Figures in brackets represent % age.

**Table—5.28: Causes of not heading family among aged men**

| *Causes* | *Pensioner (N = 32)* | *Others (N = 10)* | *Total (N = 42)* |
|---|---|---|---|
| Voluntarily handed over the responsibility because of old age | 15 (46.88) | – | 15 (35.71) |
| Frustration in familial life | 6 (18.75) | 2 (20.00) | 8 (19.05) |
| Disinheriting the authority from me by my son | 11 (34.38) | 8 (80.00) | 19 (45.24) |

*Note:* Figures in brackets represent % age.

**Table—5.29: No. of aged women managing home**

| *Category* | *Managing* | *Not managing* | *Total* |
|---|---|---|---|
| Family-pension holders | 7 (33.33) | 14 (66.67) | 21 (100.00) |
| Housewives | 23 (38.33) | 37 (61.67) | 60 (100.00) |
| **Total** | **30 (37.04)** | **51 (62.96)** | **81 (100.00)** |

*Note:* Figures in brackets represent % age.

**Table—5.30: Causes of not managing home among aged women**

| *Causes* | *FPHs (N = 14)* | *HWs (N = 37)* | *Total (N = 51)* |
|---|---|---|---|
| Voluntarily handed over the responsibility because of old age | 1 (7.14) | 5 (13.51) | 6 (11.76) |
| Frustration in familial life | 3 (21.43) | 4 (10.81) | 7 (13.73) |
| Interference of my son/s to hand over the authority to daughter-in-law | 5 (35.71) | 11 (29.73) | 16 (31.37) |
| Disinheriting the authority from me by daughter/s-in-law | 5 (35.71) | 17 (45.95) | 22 (43.14) |

*Note:* Figures in brackets represent % age.

**Table—5.31: Children consulting aged parents during crisis/difficult situations**

| *Variables* | *Pensioners* | *FPHs/HWs* | *Others* | *Total* |
|---|---|---|---|---|
| Consult | 41<br>(74.55) | 50<br>(61.73) | 4<br>(33.33) | 95<br>(64.19) |
| Do not consult | 14<br>(25.45) | 31<br>(38.27) | 8<br>(66.67) | 53<br>(35.81) |
| **Total** | **55**<br>**(100.00)** | **81**<br>**(100.00)** | **12**<br>**(100.00)** | **148** |

*Note:* Figures in brackets represent % age.

**Table—5.32: Membership of aged men in village community**

| *Answers* | *Total cases* | *% age* |
|---|---|---|
| Yes | 13 | 19.40 |
| No | 54 | 80.60 |
| **Total** | **67** | **100.00** |

**Table—5.33: Participation of aged men-members and non-members in decision-making at village meetings**

| *Variables* | *Members* | *Non-members* | *Total* |
|---|---|---|---|
| Participate | 4<br>(30.77) | 6<br>(11.11) | 10<br>(14.93) |
| Do not participate | 9<br>(69.23) | 48<br>(88.89) | 57<br>(85.07) |
| **Total** | **13**<br>**(100.00)** | **54**<br>**(100.00)** | **67**<br>**(100.00)** |

*Note:* Figures in brackets represent % age.

**Table—5.34: Acceptance of decision made by aged members in village meetings**

| *Variables* | *Total cases* | *% age* |
|---|---|---|
| Most of the times accepted | 3 | 30.00 |
| Sometimes accepted | 3 | 30.00 |
| In rare cases accepted | 4 | 40.00 |
| **Total** | **10** | **100.00** |

**Table—5.35: Members thinking aged men and women as social burden**

| | *Men* | | | *Women* | | | |
|---|---|---|---|---|---|---|---|
| | *Pensioners* | *Others* | *Total* | *FPHs* | *WHs* | *Total* | *G. total* |
| Son | – (16.67) | 2 (2.99) | 2 | – (1.67) | 1 (1.23) | 1 (2.03) | 3 |
| Spouse | 1 (1.82) | – | 1 (1.49) | – | – | – | 1 (0.68) |
| Son's wife | 5 (9.09) | 3 (25.00) | 8 (11.94) | 4 (19.5) | 12 (20.00) | 16 (19.75) | 24 (16.21) |
| Nobody | 32 (58.18) | – | 32 (47.76) | 6 (28.57) | 30 (50.00) | 36 (44.44) | 68 (45.95) |
| Do not know/ No answer | 17 (30.91) | 7 (58.33) | 24 (35.82) | 11 (52.28) | 17 (28.33) | 28 (34.57) | 52 (35.14) |
| **Total** | **55 (100.00)** | **12 (100.00)** | **67 (100.00)** | **21 (100.00)** | **60 (100.00)** | **81 (100.00)** | **148 (100.00)** |

*Note:* Figures in brackets represent % age.

**Table—5.36: Distribution of aged according to food habit**

| *Variables* | *Men* | *Women* | *Total* |
|---|---|---|---|
| Vegetarian | 4 (5.97) | 24 (29.63) | 28 (18.92) |
| Non-vegetarian | 63 (94.03) | 57 (70.37) | 120 (81.08) |
| **Total** | **67 (100.00)** | **81 (100.00)** | **148 (100.00)** |

*Note:* Figures in brackets represent % age.

**Table—5.37: Most favourite food of the aged men and women**

| Food items | *Men* | | | *Women* | | | *Total* |
|---|---|---|---|---|---|---|---|
| | *Pensioner* | *Others* | *Total* | *FPHs* | *HWs* | *Total* | |
| Fish | 6 (10.91) | 3 (25.00) | 9 (13.43) | 2 (9.52) | 10 (16.67) | 12 (14.81) | 21 (14.19) |
| Meat/ chicken | 6 (25.45) | 3 (25.00) | 9 (13.43) | 2 (9.52) | 5 (8.33) | 7 (8.64) | 16 (10.81) |
| Egg | 3 (5.45) | – | 3 (4.48) | 1 (4.76) | 2 (3.33) | 3 (3.70) | 6 (4.05) |
| Milk | 14 (25.45) | 4 (33.33) | 18 (26.87) | 4 (19.05) | 8 (13.33) | 12 (14.81) | 30 (30.27) |
| Cheese | 3 (5.45) | – | 3 (4.48) | 1 (4.76) | – | 1 (1.23) | 4 (2.70) |
| Sweet/ snacks | 8 (14.55) | 1 | 9 (13.43) | 3 (14.29) | 1 (1.67) | 4 (4.94) | 13 (8.78) |
| Mango | 7 (12.73) | – | 7 (10.45) | 1 (4.76) | 2 (3.33) | 3 (3.70) | 10 (6.76) |
| No specific item | 8 (14.55) | 1 (8.33) | 9 (13.43) | 7 (33.33) | 32 (53.33) | 39 (48.15) | 48 (32.43) |
| **Total** | **55 (100.00)** | **12 (100.00)** | **67 (100.00)** | **21 (100.00)** | **60 (100.00)** | **81 (100.00)** | **148 (100.00)** |

*Note:* Figures in brackets represent % age.

**Table—5.38: Provision of most favourite food for aged men and women**

| *Variable* | *Men* | | | *Women* | | | *Total* |
|---|---|---|---|---|---|---|---|
| | *Pensioners* | *Others* | *Total* | *FPHs* | *HWs* | *Total* | |
| Whenever you want | 1<br>(2.12) | – | 1<br>(1.72) | 2<br>(11.76) | 3<br>(7.32) | 5<br>(5.17) | 6 |
| Most frequently | 7<br>(14.89) | – | 7<br>(12.07) | 4<br>(23.53) | 3<br>(7.32) | 7<br>(12.07) | 14<br>(12.07) |
| Frequently | 6<br>(12.77) | – | 6<br>(10.34) | 2<br>(11.76) | 6<br>(14.63) | 8<br>(13.78) | 14<br>(12.07) |
| Occasionally | 10<br>(21.28) | 3<br>(27.27) | 13<br>(22.41) | 4<br>(23.53) | 3<br>(7.32) | 7<br>(12.07) | 20<br>(17.24) |
| In rare cases | 20<br>(42.55) | 5<br>(45.45) | 25<br>(43.10) | 2<br>(11.76) | 14<br>(34.15) | 16<br>(27.59) | 41<br>(35.34) |
| Not at all | 3<br>(6.38) | 3<br>(27.27) | 6<br>(10.34) | 3<br>(17.65) | 11<br>(26.83) | 14<br>(24.14) | 20<br>(17.24) |
| **Total** | **47**<br>**(100.00)** | **11**<br>**(100.00)** | **58**<br>**(100.00)** | **17**<br>**(100.00)** | **41**<br>**(100.00)** | **58**<br>**(100.00)** | **116**<br>**(100.00)** |

*Note:* Figures in brackets represent % age.

**Table—5.39: Satisfaction of aged on their daily food**

| | *Men* | | | *Women* | | | *Total* |
|---|---|---|---|---|---|---|---|
| *Variables* | *Pensioners* | *Others* | *Total* | *FPHs* | *HWs* | *Total* | |
| Fully satisfied | 15 (27.27) | 2 (16.67) | 17 (25.37) | 11 (52.38) | 18 (30.00) | 29 (20.57) | 46 (31.08) |
| Partly satisfied | 22 (40.00) | 8 (66.67) | 30 (44.78) | 8 (38.10) | 34 (56.67) | 42 (29.79) | 72 (48.65) |
| Not satisfied | 18 (32.73) | 2 (16.67) | 20 (29.85) | 2 (9.52) | 8 (13.33) | 10 (7.09) | 30 (20.27) |
| **Total** | **55 (100.00)** | **12 (100.00)** | **67 (100.00)** | **21 (100.00)** | **60 (100.00)** | **81 (100.00)** | **148 (100.00)** |

*Note:* Figures in brackets represent % age.

**Table—5.40: Narcotic habit and alcoholism among aged men and women**

| | *Men* | | | *Women* | | | *Total* |
|---|---|---|---|---|---|---|---|
| *Variables* | *Pensioners* | *Others* | *Total* | *FPHs* | *HWs* | *Total* | |
| Addicted | 43 (78.18) | 9 (75.0) | 52 (77.61) | 15 (71.43) | 43 (71.67) | 58 (71.60) | 110 (74.32) |
| Not addicted | 12 (21.82) | 3 (25.0) | 15 (22.39) | 6 (28.57) | 17 (28.33) | 23 (28.40) | 38 (25.68) |
| **Total** | **55 (100.00)** | **12 (100.00)** | **67 (100.00)** | **21 (100.00)** | **60 (100.00)** | **81 (100.00)** | **148 (100.00)** |

*Note:* Figures in brackets represent % age.

**Table—5.41: Distribution of aged according to type of addiction**

| *Items* | *Men* | | | *Women* | | | *G. Total* |
|---|---|---|---|---|---|---|---|
| | *Pensioners* (N = 43) | *Others* (N = 9) | *Total* (N = 52) | *FPHs* (N = 15) | *HWs* (N = 43) | *Total* (N = 58) | (N = 110) |
| Alcohal | 2 (4.65) | – | 2 (3.85) | – | – | – | 2 (1.82) |
| *Bidi* | 16 (26.39) | 6 (66.67) | 22 (42.31) | – | – | – | 22 (20.0) |
| Betel | 14 (32.56) | 4 (44.44) | 18 (34.62) | 12 (80.00) | 26 (60.47) | 38 (65.52) | 56 (50.91) |
| Ganja | 2 (4.65) | 2 (22.22) | 4 (7.69) | – | – | – | 4 (3.64) |
| *Khaini* | 3 (6.98) | 1 (11.11) | 4 (7.69) | 1 (6.67) | – | 1 (1.72) | 5 (4.55) |
| *Tamakhu* | 15 (34.88) | 5 (55.56) | 20 (38.46) | 10 (66.67) | 18 (41.86) | 28 (48.28) | 48 (43.64) |

*Note:* Figures in brackets represent % age.

**Table—5.42: Physical fitness among aged men and women**

| *Variables* | *Men* | *Women* | *Total* |
|---|---|---|---|
| Quite mobile without the help of anybody | 31 (46.27) | 58 (71.60) | 89 (60.14) |
| Fairly mobile without the help of walking-stick | 18 (26.87) | 11 (13.58) | 29 (19.59) |
| Fairly mobile with the help of walking-stick | 12 (17.91) | 7 (8.64) | 19 (12.84) |
| Slightly mobile with the help of an assistant | 3 (4.48) | 3 (3.70) | 6 (4.05) |
| Immobile/bedridden | 3 (4.48) | 2 (2.47) | 5 (3.38) |
| **Total** | **67 (100.00)** | **81 (100.00)** | **148 (100.00)** |

*Note:* Figures in brackets represent % age.

**Table—5.43: No. of aged suffering from at least one disease**

| *Category* | *Suffering* | *Not suffering* | *Total* |
|---|---|---|---|
| Pensioners | 50 (90.91) | 5 (9.09) | 55 (100.00) |
| Family-pension holders | 19 (90.48) | 2 (9.52) | 21 (100.00) |
| Housewives | 49 (81.67) | 11 (18.33) | 60 (100.00) |
| Others | 12 (100.00) | – | 12 (100.00) |
| **Total** | **130 (87.84)** | **18 (12.16)** | **148 (100.00)** |

*Note:* Figures in brackets represent % age.

**Table—5.44: Name of the diseases among diseased aged men and women**

| *Sl. No.* | *Disease* | *Men (N = 62)* | *Women (N = 68)* | *Total (N = 130)* |
|---|---|---|---|---|
| *(1)* | *(2)* | *(3)* | *(4)* | *(5)* |
| 1. | Asthma | 11<br>(17.74) | 8<br>(11.76) | 19<br>(14.62) |
| 2. | High blood pressure | 14<br>(22.58) | 11<br>(14.18) | 25<br>(19.23) |
| 3. | Low blood pressure | 2<br>(3.22) | 1<br>(1.67) | 3<br>(2.31) |
| 4. | Weak eye sight | 14<br>(22.58) | 12<br>(17.65) | 26<br>(20.00) |
| 5. | Cough and cold | 7<br>(11.29) | 6<br>(8.82) | 13<br>(10.00) |
| 6. | Colic/peptic ulcer | – | 2<br>(2.94) | 2<br>(1.59) |
| 7. | Constipation | 15<br>(24.19) | 8<br>(11.76) | 23<br>(17.69) |
| 8. | Diabetes | 9<br>(14.51) | 2<br>(2.94) | 11<br>(8.46) |
| 9. | Forgetfulness | 5<br>(8.06) | 3<br>(4.41) | 8<br>(6.15) |
| 10. | Filaria | 3<br>(4.84) | 1<br>(1.47) | 4<br>(3.08) |
| 11. | Gastric | 7<br>(11.29) | 5<br>(7.35) | 12<br>(9.23) |
| 12. | Giddiness | 7<br>(11.29) | 6<br>(8.82) | 13<br>(10.0) |
| 13. | Heart problem | 6<br>(9.68) | 4<br>(5.88) | 10<br>(7.69) |
| 14. | Hearing problem | 3<br>(4.84) | 3<br>(4.41) | 6<br>(4.62) |
| 15. | Hydrocele | 1<br>(1.61) | – | 1<br>(0.77) |
| 16. | Loss of speech | 7<br>(11.29) | 2<br>(2.94) | 9<br>(6.92) |
| 17. | Paralysis | 2<br>(3.23) | 1<br>(1.47) | 3<br>(2.31) |

*(Contd...)*

| *(1)* | *(2)* | *(3)* | *(4)* | *(5)* |
|---|---|---|---|---|
| 18. | Parkinson | 1<br>(1.61) | – | 1<br>(6.77) |
| 19. | Piles | 3<br>(4.84) | 4<br>(5.88) | 7<br>(5.38) |
| 20. | Rheumatism | 13<br>(29.03) | 9<br>(13.24) | 27<br>(20.77) |
| 21. | Urinary problem | 3<br>(4.84) | 1<br>(1.47) | 4<br>(3.08) |
| 22. | Waist/back pain | 3<br>(4.84) | 3<br>(4.41) | 6<br>(4.62) |

*Note:* Figures in brackets represent % age.

**Table—5.45: Treatment of aged men and women**

| | *Men* | | | *Women* | | | *Total* |
|---|---|---|---|---|---|---|---|
| *Variables* | *Pensioners* | *Others* | *Total* | *FPHs* | *HWs* | *Total* | |
| *(1)* | *(2)* | *(3)* | *(4)* | *(5)* | *(6)* | *(7)* | *(8)* |
| Undergoing treatment | 17<br>(34.00) | 2<br>(16.67) | 19<br>(30.65) | 5<br>(26.32) | 4<br>(8.16) | 9<br>(13.24) | 28<br>(21.54) |
| Not under-going any treatment | 33<br>(66.67) | 10<br>(83.33) | 43<br>(69.35) | 14<br>(73.68) | 45<br>(91.84) | 59<br>(86.76) | 102<br>(78.46) |
| **Total** | **50**<br>**(100.00)** | **12**<br>**(100.00)** | **62**<br>**(100.00)** | **19**<br>**(100.00)** | **49**<br>**(100.00)** | **68**<br>**(100.00)** | **130**<br>**(100.00)** |

*Note:* Figures in brackets represent % age.

**Table—5.46: Type of treatment among aged diseased men and women**

| *Type of treatment* | *Men* | | | *Women* | | | *Total* |
|---|---|---|---|---|---|---|---|
| | *Pensioners* | *Others* | *Total* | *FPHs* | *HWs* | *Total* | |
| *(1)* | *(2)* | *(3)* | *(4)* | *(5)* | *(6)* | *(7)* | *(8)* |
| Allopathic | 14 (82.35) | – | 14 (73.68) | 3 (60.00) | 3 (75.00) | 6 (66.62) | 20 (71.43) |
| Homoeopathic | 1 (5.88) | 2 (100.00) | 3 (15.79) | 2 (40.00) | – | 2 (22.22) | 5 (17.86) |
| Ayurvedic | 2 (11.76) | – | 2 (10.53) | – | 1 (25.00) | 1 (11.11) | 3 (10.71) |
| **Total** | **17 (100.00)** | **12 (100.00)** | **19 (100.00)** | **5 (100.00)** | **4 (100.00)** | **9 (100.00)** | **28 (100.00)** |

*Note:* Figures in brackets represent % age.

**Table—5.47: Bearer of the cost of the treatment of the aged men and women**

| *Bearers* | *Pensioners* | *FPHs* | *Housewives* | *Others* | *Total* |
|---|---|---|---|---|---|
| *(1)* | *(2)* | *(3)* | *(4)* | *(5)* | *(6)* |
| Self | 14 (82.35) | 3 (60.0) | – | 1 (50.00) | 18 (64.29) |
| Son | – | 1 (20.00) | 1 (25.00) | 1 (50.00) | 3 (10.71) |
| Spouse | – | – | 2 (50.00) | – | 2 (7.14) |
| Self and son | 3 (17.65) | 1 (20.00) | – | – | 4 (14.29) |
| Spouse and son | – | – | 1 (25.00) | – | 1 (3.57) |
| **Total** | **17 (100.00)** | **5 (100.00)** | **4 (100.00)** | **2 (100.00)** | **28 (100.00)** |

*Note:* Figures in brackets represent % age.

**Table—5.48: Satisfaction of aged men and women on their treatment**

| *Variables* | *Pensioners* | *FPHs* | *Housewives* | *Others* | *Total* |
|---|---|---|---|---|---|
| Fully satisfied | 7<br>(41.18) | 2<br>(40.00) | – | – | 9<br>(32.14) |
| Partially satisfied | 3<br>(17.65) | 2<br>(40.00) | 3<br>(75.00) | 2<br>(100.00) | 10<br>(35.71) |
| Not satisfied | 7<br>(41.18) | 1<br>(20.00) | 1<br>(25.00) | – | 9<br>(32.14) |
| **Total** | **17**<br>**(100.00)** | **5**<br>**(100.00)** | **4**<br>**(100.00)** | **2**<br>**(100.00)** | **28**<br>**(100.00)** |

*Note:* Figures in brackets represent % age.

**Table—5.49: Do you feel loneliness?**

| | *Answer* | | *Total* |
|---|---|---|---|
| *Category of aged* | *Yes* | *No* | |
| Pensioners | 37<br>(67.27) | 18<br>(32.73) | 55<br>(100.00) |
| Family-pension holders and housewives | 22<br>(27.16) | 59<br>(72.84) | 81<br>(100.00) |
| Others | 5<br>(41.67) | 7<br>(58.33) | 12<br>(100.00) |
| **Total** | **64**<br>**(43.24)** | **84**<br>**(56.76)** | **148**<br>**(100.00)** |

*Note:* Figures in brackets represent % age.

**Table—5.50: Degree of loneliness among aged who feel lonely**

| *Category of aged* | *Degree of loneliness* | | | *Total* |
|---|---|---|---|---|
| | *To a great extent* | *To a moderate extent* | *To some extent* | |
| Pensioners | 18 (48.65) | 11 (29.73) | 8 (21.62) | 37 (100.00) |
| Family-pension holders and housewives | 3 (13.64) | 13 (59.09) | 6 (27.27) | 22 (100.00) |
| Others | 2 (40.00) | 3 (60.00) | – | 5 (100.00) |
| **Total** | **23 (35.94)** | **27 (42.19)** | **14 (21.88)** | **64 (100.00)** |

*Note:* Figures in brackets represent % age.

**Table—5.51: No. of aged having friends with whom they can share their feelings on day-to-day life**

| *Answers* | *Aged men* | *Aged women* | *Total* |
|---|---|---|---|
| *(1)* | *(2)* | *(3)* | *(4)* |
| Have | 49 (73.13) | 71 (87.65) | 120 (81.08) |
| Do not have | 18 (26.87) | 10 (12.35) | 28 (18.92) |
| **Total** | **67 (100.00)** | **81 (100.00)** | **148 (100.00)** |

*Note:* Figures in brackets represent % age.

**Table—5.52: Recreational activities of aged men and women during leisure time**

| Sl. No. | Activities | Regularly | | | Occasionally | | | Total | | |
|---|---|---|---|---|---|---|---|---|---|---|
| | | M | F | T | M | F | T | M | F | T |
| (1) | (2) | (3) | (4) | (5) | (6) | (7) | (8) | (9) | (10) | (11) |
| 1. | Reading of religious books | 18 (26.87) | 6 (7.41) | 24 (16.22) | 6 (8.90) | 3 (3.71) | 9 (6.08) | 24 (35.82) | 9 (11.11) | 39 (22.30) |
| 2. | Listening to religious recitation | 3 (4.48) | 6 (7.41) | 9 (6.08) | 11 (16.42) | 6 (7.41) | 17 (11.49) | 14 (20.9) | 12 (14.81) | 26 (17.56) |
| 3. | Reading of story books | 13 (19.40) | - | 13 (8.78) | 2 (2.99) | 1 (1.23) | 3 (2.03) | 15 (22.39) | 1 (1.23) | 16 (10.81) |
| 4. | News paper | 10 (14.93) | - | 10 (6.76) | 7 (10.45) | - | 7 (4.73) | 17 (25.37) | - | 17 (11.49) |
| 5. | Listening to radio | 11 (16.42) | 2 (2.47) | 13 (8.78) | 6 (11.94) | 5 (6.17) | 13 (8.78) | 19 (28.36) | 7 (8.64) | 26 (17.57) |
| 6. | Watching T.V. | 14 (20.9) | 7 (8.64) | 21 (14.19) | 7 (10.45) | 7 (8.64) | 14 (9.46) | 21 (31.34) | 14 (17.28) | 35 (23.65) |
| 7. | Viewing cinema at film halls | - | - | - | 1 (1.49) | - | 1 (0.68) | 1 (1.49) | - | 1 (0.68) |
| 8. | Playing cards | 21 (31.34) | 11 (13.58) | 32 (21.62) | 17 (25.37) | 06 (7.41) | 23 (15.54) | 38 (56.72) | 17 (20.99) | 55 (37.16) |

(Contd...)

| (1) | (2) | (3) | (4) | (5) | (6) | (7) | (8) | (9) | (10) | (11) |
|---|---|---|---|---|---|---|---|---|---|---|
| 9. | Playing *Pasa* | 3 (4.48) | – | 3 (2.03) | 2 (2.99) | – | 2 (1.35) | 5 (7.46) | – | 5 (3.38) |
| 10. | Gossiping/spending time at village tea stall/meeting pandal | 17 (25.37) | – | 17 (11.49) | 30 (44.78) | – | – | 47 (70.15) | – | 47 (31.76) |
| 11. | Simply sitting at home | 16 (23.88) | 9 (13.43) | 15 (10.14) | – | – | – | 16 (23.88) | 9 (11.11) | 25 (16.89) |
| 12. | Morning walk | 4 (5.97) | – | 4 (2.70) | – | – | – | 4 (5.97) | – | 4 (2.70) |

*Note:* Figures in brackets represent % age.

**Table—5.53: Drawal of pension from different sources**

| *Category* | *Treasury* | *Public Banks* | *Total* |
|---|---|---|---|
| Pensioners | 43<br>(78.18) | 12<br>(21.82) | 55<br>(100.00) |
| Family-pension holders | 17<br>(80.95) | 4<br>(19.05) | 21<br>(100.00) |
| **Total** | **60**<br>**(78.95)** | **16**<br>**(21.05)** | **76**<br>**(100.00)** |

*Note:* Figures in brackets represent % age.

6

# Constitutional Safeguards, Welfare Measures and Recommendations

## CONSTITUTIONAL SAFEGUARDS AND WELFARE MEASURES

Every person of independent India has the right to live. This has been ensured by the constitution of India. It provides for some meaningful duties to the state governments to safeguard the basic interests of the senior citizens of our nation. The duties of the state governments have been clearly spelt out in the Directive Principles of State Policies vide Article 41 of the constitution that "enjoins on the State to make effective provisions within the limits of its economic capacity and development for public assistance in case of unemployment, old age, sickness and disablement and in other cases of undeserved want" (G.O.I, 1993: 2). In order to make this provision effective, the responsibility for providing relief to the disabled/unemployable aged persons, is explained in the State List of the 'Seventh Schedule' of the Constitution and the subjects like social security and social insurance, employment and unemployment have been mentioned in the concurrent list of the 'Seventh Schedule' with a view to providing necessary assistance to the aged and other such persons (cf. ibid). With a view to making these provisions fruitful, both the State Government and Union Government have formulated various welfare measures for the well-being of the aged people. Such welfare schemes/programmes mainly run by the voluntary organisations with formal financial assistance from the respective governments. Presently, there are five major welfare schemes of the Union Government which are in operation in the country through different state governments.

Apart from the scheme of the Union Government, many states have their own welfare for the betterment of these people. Now, the Government of Orissa has two such schemes which run out of its own funds. The individual welfare schemes of the Union Government and Government of Orissa are described below:

## WELFARE SCHEMES OF THE UNION GOVERNMENT

The welfare schemes of the Union Government which are in operation for the well-being of the aged people of the country are as follows:

*(i)* National Social Assistance Programme (NSAP);

*(ii)* Foster care/adoption services for the aged;

*(iii)* Mobile medicare services for the aged;

*(iv)* Day-care centres for the aged; and

*(v)* Old-age homes (Maintenance and Services of Old-Age Homes).

### (i) National Social Assistance Programme (NSAP)

This programme is in operation in the country with effect from 15th August, 1995. It constitutes three specific sectoral schemes namely (a) National Old-Age Pension Scheme (NOAPS), (b) National Family Benefit Scheme (NFBS) and (c) National Maternity Benefit Scheme (NMBS). But the former two schemes are directly linked with the welfare of the aged people of the nation.

#### *(a) National Old-Age Pension Scheme (NOAPS)*

As per the guidelines of National Social Assistance Programme (NSAP) of Government of India, under National Old-Age Pension Scheme (NOAS), an amount of Rs. 75/- is provided to an aged person per month who is 65-years-old provided that he/she is a destitute in the sense of having little or no regular means of subsistence from his/her own spouse or financial support from family members or other sources. Presently the Government of Orissa is providing this assistance to a total number of 3,33,400 beneficiaries under this scheme at the rate of Rs. 100/- per month per beneficiary, i.e., with an additional assistance of Rs. 25/- per month per beneficiary to the original assistance of Rs. 75/- per month per beneficiary of the Government of India. Thus, Government of Orissa has been very kind to increase the assistance of Rs. 75/- of Government of India to Rs. 100/- by voluntarily meeting an amount of Rs. 25/- per beneficiary per month out of its own fund. This has certainly been made with a view to equalising the amount of pension of both the Central and State schemes. (District-wise target of pensioners under national old-age pension scheme in Orissa (1998-99) is presented in Appendix 10).

***(b) National Family Benefit Scheme (NFBS)***

This is a scheme in which some family benefit for the households below the poverty line is provided on the death of the primary breadwinner in the bereaved family subject to the guidelines for assistance.

*(i)* The 'Primary breadwinner' will be the member of the household—male of female, whose earnings contribute the largest proportion to the total household income.

*(ii)* The death of such a primary breadwinner should have occurred whilst he/or she is in the age group of 18 to 64 years, i.e., more than 18 years and less than 65 years of age.

*(iii)* Rs. 5,000 in the case of death due to natural causes of Rs. 10,000 in the case of death due to accidental cases will be the ceilings for the purpose of claiming Central assistance (G.O.I, 1995: 7-8).

The family benefits are paid to such member/s of the household of the deceased who, after local enquiry is/are determined to be the head of the household. For the purpose of the scheme, the term 'household' includes spouse, minor children, unmarried daughters and dependent parents (cf. Ibid p. 8).

Thus, from the above determining factors, it is learnt that if an aged person who is either a male or female dies naturally or unnaturally when he/she is the main breadwinner, his/her spouse or dependent parents or others are entitled to get the assistance depending upon the legal procedures pertaining to their succession.

**(ii) Foster Care/Adoption Services for the Aged**

Under this programme various social services are provided to the homeless and lonely old people who lead a pitiable life because of utter poverty and helplessness. Arrangement is made to place such aged persons with the willing families considering to the local culture and social values of either parties.

**(iii) Mobile Medicare Services for the Aged**

Mobile medicare service is a very useful scheme for the aged people who reside in rural and in urban slums. Many of them suffer from various age-based diseases and remain untreated because of poverty. So, under this programme, medical consultation and treatment facilities are rendered to such people through mobile health camps by trained medical experts.

Presently, under this scheme there are only three mobile medical centres in the State of Orissa of which two are running in Bhubaneswar city and the rest one in Sagargaon, Khurdha, through 3 different non-government organisations (NGOs). One of these three units has started functioning from April 1994, another from September, 1998, and the rest one from December, 1998 (Appendix 11). Hence, this service is reached to a few patients confined to Khurdha district only.

**(iv) Day-care Centres for the Aged**

The main purpose of this scheme' is to keep the aged integrated in their respective families and to supplement the activities of the family in looking after the needs of the aged. Both groups of the aged, viz, well-to-do and the poor in the age group of 60 years and above should benefit from the programme" (G.O.I., 1995: 9).

In order to fulfil these objectives of the scheme, financial assistance is provided to the NGO sectors for maintenance of 'Day-Care Centres' for the aged belonging to urban, urban slums, rural and tribal pockets of the State.

The guidelines which are specified by the Government of India for working of day-care centres for the aged are as follows:

*(a)* The activities of a day-care centre should be such as would lead to improve in the living styles and gainful utilisation of the spare time of the elderly persons.

*(b)* A day-care centre shall establish links with welfare institutions and welfare services available to various categories of people in the area and make efforts to involve its members in those activities and services.

*(c)* Every day-care centre shall have activities of interest to its members and to the elders living in the area and ensure participation of elderly in these activities.

*(d)* A day-care centre should have at least 150 aged persons in their list, so that even after dropout and absenteeism, its daily attendance does not fall below 50. Thus, a day-care centre should run at a strength of 50 aged persons.

*(e)* It should have duly satisfied regular timings with a minimum of 4 hours at scheduled activities in a day. The activities include gainful activities, discussions, discourses, adult education, health education, counselling/social work, games, outings etc.

*(f)* A day-care centre should have adequate accommodation (at least two 4 x 5 m rooms) and seating arrangements.

*(g)* A trained social worker with the minimum qualification of graduation degree in social work from a recognised university with one year experience in social work, counselling, medical and psychiatric social work or a person with M.A. degree in social work, psychology, sociology should be appointed in

urban areas. The day-care centres located in tribal/rural/slum areas should appoint an organiser/supervisor with a minimum qualification of a graduation or post-graduation degree in social work, sociology, anthropology or any other social science.

*(h)* Each day-care centre should appoint a part-time qualified physician for medical check-up of the aged persons. Cases which require further medical care should be referred to the nearby government hospitals. The organisation should incur a limited expenditure for medicines which serve as first aid.

*(i)* The organisation should utilise the community services available in the area for running day-care centres. For such facilities, they should approach the concerned state government/local authorities in advance for getting such provisions to run the day-care centre. The ministry would consider rent of the accommodation only if they have no such arrangements/facilities in the proposed area. In such cases, the organisation should furnished a certificate from the local authority indicating the rent of accommodation paid to the owner of the building, and

*(j)* The expenses of outings and visits shall be borne by the elderly themselves except in case of those elderly who are destitute and have no source of income (1993: 9-12).

With the above objectives and guidelines specified by the Government of India, presently a total number of 52 day care centres are running in Orissa through 27 non-government organisations (NGOs) in 13 districts namely Khurdha (18 or 34.62%), Dhenkanal (8 or 15.38%), Angul (7 or 13.46%), Jajpur (5 or 9.62%), Puri (5 or 9.62%), Kenderapara (2 or 3.85%), Bhawanipatna (1 or 1.96%), Cuttack (1 or 1.92%), Ganjam (1.92%), Koraput (1 or 1.96%), Nayagarh (1 or 1.92%), Nuapada (1 or 1.92%) and Rayagada (1 or 1.92%). These day care centres provide the assistance within the limit of the scheme to a total number of 7800 aged persons at the rate of 150 beneficiaries per centre (Table 6.1). Of the total 52 day care centres maximum, i.e. 170 (32.69%) have commenced functioning in the state only in 1998 (Table 6.2). However, this scheme is limited to only 13 districts and the discrepancies prevailed are very conspicuous since there is no uniformity in coverage of day care centres in each district of the state. When in Khurdha, Dhenkanal, Angul, Jajpur and Puri more or less 10 per cent of the total number of centres run, in each of the remaining districts there is only one centre. (Name and district-wise NGOs running day care centres are presented in Appendix 12).

**(v) Old-Age Homes (Maintenance and Services of Old-Age Homes)**

Under this scheme, poor and destitute aged persons of 60 years are accommodated in old-age homes. The destitute and helpless aged persons belonging to lower middle income groups are also covered under the scheme provided that they meet the eligibility conditions. The inmates of old-age homes are kept in a familial environment and the social workers and counsellors take utmost care. Their physical and psychological well-being are also taken care of with assistance of the trained medical professionals. Medicines upto limited extent are also provided with a view to making the diseased and psychologically depressed old persons fit to face the situations and to lead the rest of their life in peace.

As per the latest figure available from the government, presently a total number of 26 old-age homes are in operation in 14 districts of the state (Table 6.3). These 26 old-age homes run through 25 voluntary organisations (Appendix 13). Apart from these, there are two old-age homes which run with the financial assistance from Government of Orissa. (Appendix 14).

Table 6.3 speaks that of the total 26 old-age homes, highest number of homes, i.e., 6 (23.08%) run in the district of Puri followed by 5 (19.23%) homes in Khurdha, 2 (7.69%) each in the district of Angul, Kenderapara and Phulbani. In each of the rest district, viz, Bhawanipatna, Bolangir, Cuttack, Dhenkanal, Ganjam, G. Udaygiri, Jagatsinghpur, Koraput and Nuapada, there is only one old-age home.

Normally, an old-age home provides shelter for 25 aged destitute. Hence all the 26 old-age homes provides shelter for 650 aged persons of the state. This otherwise shows that when in the district of Puri 150 aged persons take benefit out of it, it is 125 in Khurdha, 50 each in Angul, Kendrapara and Phulbani depending upon the number of old-age homes available in these districts. Each of the rest districts provides benefit to only 25 aged persons (Table 6.3).

So far as the commencement of the old-age home facility for the destitute age persons of the state is concerned, it started in 1990 with 2 old-age homes but highest percentage of homes started functioning only in the last year, i.e., 1998 (Table 6.4).

## WELFARE SCHEMES OF THE GOVT. OF ORISSA

For the welfare of the aged people of the State of Orissa, government of Orissa implement two specific scheme, namely, 'Old-Age Pension' and 'Old-Age Home' out of its own fund. The details of these schemes are as follows:

### *(a) Old-Age Pension Scheme*

Old-age pension scheme was introduced by the Government of Orissa on 25th March, 1975 vide Resolution No. 12066/Pen. 30-74 F and the scheme came into force on the 1st April, 1975. Further in 1985, the widows aged 50 or above and in 1989, the leprosy patients aged 60 or more with visible signs of deformity were also included in the scheme.

As far as Notification 1246, dated the 10th September 1990, the Government of Orissa has fixed of Rs. 100/- per month per aged person as pension. This amount has been provided to such persons with effect from 2nd October, 1990. The eligibility conditions for the award of pension under Amended Rule-5 of the resolution are as follows:

*(a)* *(i)* He/she is of 65-years of age or above;

*(ii)* Or a widow irrespective of age;

*(iii)* Or a small farmer/marginal farmer or a landless agricultural labourer of 60-years of age or above;

(*b*) His/her income does not exceed Rs. 3200 per annum. (vide Resolution 9726-ISD-24/90/PR, dated the 9th October, 1990).

(*c*) Has nobody to support;

(*d*) Is a permanent resident of Orissa;

(*e*) has not been convicted of on criminal offence; and

(*f*) Is not in receipt of any assistance from the government, State or Central or any organisation aided by either government.

Presently (1998-99), the Government of Orissa is providing old-age pension to a total number of 5,28,000 beneficiaries at the rate of Rs. 100/- per aged person per month out of its own fund. District-wise number of pensioners is mentioned in Appendix 15.

### (*b*) *Old-Age Homes*

Government of Orissa is operating only 2 old-age homes through local NGOs out of its own fund. One old-age home is operating at Raghunathpur of Jagatsinghpur district and the other at Nimapara N.A.C. of Puri district (Appendix. 14). Each of these old-age homes render assistance within the objectives, to a total number of 25 aged persons irrespective of sex.

## RECOMMENDATIONS

Basing on different problems and welfare measures of the government, the following recommendations are made under different broad headlines with a view to facilitating better living standard for the aged. The recommendations are mainly made on the basis of different social perspectives and on the modes and ways of functioning of government schemes.

### (*a*) *Social Perspectives*

(*i*) In Hindu India, generally there are two types of traditional system of land-transfer from parental to filial generations. These are *Dayabhag* and *Mitakshyara*. The former system is prevalent in Bengal, Assam and Tripura and the latter one in Orissa and other parts of the country.

According to *Dayabhag* system, so long as the father is alive, he is the sole authority of all the landed properties he has with him, and in that case he enjoys the absolute right and freedom to dispose off his land in any manner to anybody depending upon his own choice and interest. However, he may donate his lands to his son/s if he is satisfied with him/them or he may give a part of it to him/them out of his *Daya* or sense of humanity. Hence, the progenies cannot claim a right over ancestral land or immovable properties. But *Mitakshyar* is a system that goes almost against the ethics of *Dayabhag*. In this system, ancient or paternal landed properties and automatically inherited by the progenies and hence, a person cannot sell or donate his paternal properties legally without the prior consent of his son/s. But he has every right to manage, sell or donate the landed properties he has generated within his own lifetime out of his own efforts and resources.

Thus, in societies where the system of *Dayabhag* is prevalent, the aged parents are respected, honoured and their authority in family is highly acknowledged with due respect and reverence and in such societies they are to get the landed properties from their parents. So, this traditional system seems to be an outweigh as a system of social insurance for leading life smoothly during old age. As a result, this system needs to be legalised in places where the system of *Mitakshyar* is prevalent. This would be effectively done only by the active intervention of the government through proper modification of existing land-rules on inheritance of landed properties.

*(ii)* Parents labour hard to get their children educated and employed. But in many cases the employed children do not support their old parents financially. So, the employed children, particularly sons must give a particular proportion of their income to their parents for maintenance every month. The proportion of the income of sons to be given should be calculated as per the following formula:

Total income of son divided by total number of family members (including parents) and the per capita share be handed over to the parents officially by deducting from the salary of son/s. This would certainly reduced the financial burden of the aged for self-management during their inactive period.

**(b) Welfare Perspectives**

(i) India is primarily an agricultural country. A large chunk of rural people contribute their labour for improving the productivity of land and hence Indian economy is based on the rural labour force. Once they stop working, the whole country may be paralysed. But their condition has been very miserable since time immemorial and the welfare measures available for them is very meagre. The get old-age pension but the amount is very low (i.e., Rs. 100/- per mouth per person w.e.f 1990) as compared to the service holders. When in the present time, the daily wage of a skilled labourer is fixed at Rs. 42/- per day, the provision of Rs. 100/- per month per an aged person is nothing but a drop in an ocean. Another factor which catches the mind of general public is that the salary or pension of government officials or retired persons is enhanced according to the price index at a specified time interval with a view to cooping with the changing economy, but no impressive action has been taken to raise the amount of old-age pension according to the price index of daily commodities So, it destitute aged persons are to lead a very woeful life even if their contribution to youth labour force is well recognised for the growth of Indian economy. Government machinery must think in this perspective and necessary steps be taken to increase the amount of old-age pension. Government, may get the extra amount from its employees, especially from the tax payers by deducting a token amount from their salary every month for the welfare of the aged citizens. This could the effectively be done through sustained interest and action.

*(ii)* Presently there are only 8 lead banks namely State Bank of India, United Commercial Bank, Bank of India, Indian Overseas Bank, Indian Bank, Central Bank, United Bank of India and Commercial Bank through which pension transactions are made. But pension transactions should be made through all the nationalised banks and even Gramya Banks. This would ensure easy drawal of pension from any nearest bank and hence, the aged would get relieved from the painstaking and difficult task of coming over to treasuries physically every month for drawal of their pension or arrears.

*(iii)* Sitting arrangement must be provided within the premises of treasuries as the aged face a lot of problems. They need rest as they are old and feeble. Some facilities ought to be provided to them.

*(iv)* The existing treasuries are functioning on the first floor of the treasury buildings. It creates many problems for a number of aged persons to climb up. If treasuries function on the ground floor, it would be advantageous for the pensioners.

*(v)* Different dates have been specified by the treasuries for drawal of monthly pension and drawal of arrears. For this, an aged has to come twice if he/she has any arrear to get. So, arrears must be paid to the aged pensioners on the date of drawal of monthly pensions.

*(vi)* Prior to 1987, drawal of pension by money order was available for the aged and the delivery charges were being born by the government. But when on 1st August, 1987 the minimum pension and family-pension was raised to Rs. 300/- per month, delivery of pension by money order was discontinued in order to reduce the financial burden of the government. This facility renewed. In order to avoid false delivery, the village committee be involved in the process of identification of pensioners of family-pension holding

beneficiaries and the said committee may be kept responsible or all false deliveries if made through their involvement.

*(vii)* A fixed amount of medical allowance be given to the pensioners or family-pension holders since old-age is fraught with many age-based diseases and hence an aged requires an extra amount for treatment of diseases.

**Table—6.1: District-wise distribution of day-care centres in Orissa**

| *Sl. No.* | *District* | *No. of DCCs* | *% age* | *Total Beneficiaries* | *Average* |
|---|---|---|---|---|---|
| 1. | Angul | 7 | 13.46 | 1050 | 150 |
| 2. | Bhawanipatna | 1 | 1.92 | 150 | 150 |
| 3. | Cuttack | 1 | 1.92 | 150 | 150 |
| 4. | Dhenkanal | 8 | 15.38 | 1200 | 150 |
| 5. | Ganjam | 1 | 1.92 | 150 | 150 |
| 6. | Jajpur | 5 | 9.62 | 750 | 150 |
| 7. | Kendrapara | 2 | 3.85 | 300 | 150 |
| 8. | Khurdha | 18 | 34.62 | 2700 | 150 |
| 9. | Koraput | 1 | 1.92 | 150 | 150 |
| 10. | Nayagarh | 1 | 1.92 | 150 | 150 |
| 11. | Nuapara | 1 | 1.92 | 150 | 150 |
| 12. | Puri | 5 | 9.62 | 750 | 150 |
| 13. | Rayagada | 1 | 1.92 | 150 | 150 |
| | **Total** | **52** | **100.00** | **7800** | **150** |

**Table—6.2: Year of commencement of day-care centre in Orissa**

| *Year* | *No. of DCCs* | *% age* |
|---|---|---|
| 1979 | 5 | 9.62 |
| 1987 | 5 | 9.62 |
| 1990 | 1 | 1.92 |
| 1991 | 6 | 11.54 |
| 1992 | 3 | 5.77 |
| 1993 | 10 | 19.23 |
| 1994 | 3 | 5.77 |
| 1995 | 2 | 3.85 |
| 1998 | 17 | 32.69 |
| **Total** | **52** | **100.00** |

**Table—6.3: District-wise distribution of old-age homes in Orissa**

| *Sl. No.* | *District* | *No. of OAHs* | *% age* | *Total beneficiary* | *Average* |
|---|---|---|---|---|---|
| 1. | Angul | 2 | 7.69 | 50 | 25 |
| 2. | Bhawanipatna | 1 | 3.85 | 25 | 25 |
| 3. | Bolangir | 1 | 3.85 | 25 | 25 |
| 4. | Cuttack | 1 | 3.85 | 25 | 25 |
| 5. | Dhenkanal | 1 | 3.85 | 25 | 25 |
| 6. | Ganjam | 1 | 3.85 | 25 | 25 |
| 7. | G. Udaygiri | 1 | 3.85 | 25 | 25 |
| 8. | Jagatsinghpur | 1 | 3.85 | 25 | 25 |
| 9. | Kendrapara | 2 | 7.69 | 50 | 25 |
| 10. | Khurdha | 5 | 19.23 | 125 | 25 |
| 11. | Koraput | 1 | 3.85 | 25 | 25 |
| 12. | Naupada | 1 | 3.85 | 25 | 25 |
| 13. | Phulbani | 2 | 7.69 | 50 | 25 |
| 14. | Puri | 6 | 23.08 | 150 | 25 |
| | **Total** | **26** | **100.00** | **650** | **25** |

*Note:* Compiled from the data available from Women and Child Welfare Department, Govt. of Orissa.

**Table—6.4: Year of commencement of old-age homes in Orissa**

| *Year* | *No. of OAHs* | *% age* |
|---|---|---|
| 1990 | 2 | 7.69 |
| 1991 | 4 | 15.38 |
| 1992 | 1 | 3.84 |
| 1993 | 5 | 19.23 |
| 1994 | 3 | 11.54 |
| 1995 | 3 | 11.54 |
| 1996 | 1 | 3.85 |
| 1997 | – | – |
| 1998 | 7 | 26.92 |
| **Total** | **26** | **100.00** |

7

# Summary and Conclusion

India is now facing a number of social problems including that of the aged in the tradition-bound (rural) as well as in modern (urban) contemporary societies. In both these types of society, their problems are increasing at an alarming rate coinciding with the pace of population growth, and hence, struggle for existence is becoming very acute. In such a situation, their social standing has come down to nihility in many highly industrialised and developed nations of the world and so also in developing countries like India, where the filial generations have become very mechanical and self-centred in order to lead life independently, thereby leaving their aged parents or relatives at the back door. This circumstance, of course, compels the aged to lead a very miserable life in isolation. They suffer from various psychological traumas and in most of the cases, their mental agony and pangs of life remain obscure. This has, no doubt, made a concern for all of us to make studies on such a crucial problem and suggest remedial measures.

In the present study an attempt has been made to show the social situation of the oriya aged persons belonging to different strata of population, viz, retired government servants, family-pension holders, and non-pensioners including housewives, agriculturists, wage-earners, business men etc., who reside on the outskirts of Bhubaneswar city, the capital of Orissa.

The broad objectives of the study are as follows:

- *(i)* to find out the family type and living arrangement of the aged;
- *(ii)* to find out the nature of work participation and economic support of the aged for maintenance of house;
- *(iii)* to analyse the attitudinal behaviour and the degree of social relationship between the aged and younger generations in the family;
- *(iv)* to analyse the generation gap and decision-making process at the household and community levels;
- *(v)* to find out the food and narcotic habits of the aged;
- *(vi)* to examine the health status, treatment of diseases and mode of expenditure pattern on treatment of the aged;
- *(vii)* to examine the nature of leisure and recreational activities of the aged; and
- *(viii)* to find out the extent of problem relating to the official transaction of pension disbursement.

The results of the study are based on a sample of 148 aged persons drawn from 21 peripheral villages of Bhubaneswar city. Of these 21 villages, 12 fall in Balianta block and the rest 9 in Bhubaneswar block of Khurda district.

The main findings of the study are presented below:

**Family Type and Living Arrangement**

- *(i)* Of the total number of 148 aged, maximum, i.e., 46.62 per cent (69) live in vertically extended families followed by 33.11 per cent (49) of aged in nuclear and 18.24 per cent (27) in supplemented families. There are only 1.35 per cent (2) who belong to sub-nuclear families. The rest 0.68 per cent of one belongs to broken category.
- *(ii)* That 82.43 per cent of 122 aged live along with the members of their own generation, i.e. their spouse. The rest, have either lost their spouses or because of some other reasons, lead life without their life

partners. However, more than 87 per cent (87.16) or 129 aged lead life with the relatives of their first descending generations, viz, sons, daughters-in-law etc. But 58.78 per cent (87) of them have the kins belonging to second descending generation who are presently staying with them. The kins of this generation are mainly grandchildren.

*(iii)* So far as the family members by exact relationship are concerned, highest percentage (37.84) of the aged live with their spouses, married children and unmarried grandchildren. They are followed by 21.62 per cent (32) who live with their spouses and unmarried children. On the contrary 14.19 per cent or 21 aged live without spouse but with married sons and unmarried grandchildren. Unfortunately a total number of 17 or 11.49 per cent of aged lead a woeful life only with their spouses as there is nobody to look after them.

*(iv)* A total number of 59 or 39.86 per cent of aged opine that the living-rooms available to them (households) are sufficient for all the family members. But from amongst these persons, only 20 or 33.90 per cent have independent living-rooms and the rest do not have it. On the contrary 89 or 60.14 per cent say that the available living-rooms are insufficient for all the family members, but fortunately 13 or 14.61 per cent of them have separate living-rooms for leading life comfortably.

*(v)* In total, only 29 or 19.59 per cent of aged persons have separate living-rooms and the rest 119 or 80.41 per cent do not have it.

*(vi)* That from amongst those (119) who do not have separate living-rooms, maximum, i.e. 54 or 45.38 per cent are adjusted in any room/place depending upon the availability and situations. Next to them, 35 or 29.41 per cent living in entrance-rooms. Surprisingly 26 or 21.85 per cent of them stay in enclosed verandah

of own house and an aged accounting for 0.84 per cent, lives in an enclosed verandah of its neighbour's house. The rest one spends night in the premises of *Bhagabat ghar* (community house) of the village.

**Economic Support, and Contribution of Physical Labour towards Family**

*(i)* That most (59.21%) of the aged, particularly pensioners and family-pension holders earn in between Rs. 1000/- 1500/- per month with an average income of Rs. 1252.84 per month per person.

*(ii)* About 41 per cent of aged keep their whole income with themselves and contribute it for the management of home depending upon the requirement. But 36.84 per cent or 28 aged hand over their whole income to their son/s. The rest 22.37 per cent or 17, however, partly keep their income with themselves and give the rest to their son/s.

*(iii)* Among the non-bedridden aged men, many work in different sectors of daily chores of life. But those who frequently look after domestic animals constitute 34.38 per cent or 22 aged persons. They are followed by 32.81 per cent or 21 aged who supervise agricultural activities. About 31.00 per cent or 20 persons attend to visit the house of relatives during social functions, and 28.13 per cent or 18 of them do shopping. Next to them 26.56 per cent or 17 look after the education of their grandchildren. Those who cook food, clean utensils, house floor and clothes account for 1.56 per cent.

*(iv)* Among the non-bedridden aged women, highest percentage of them clean utensils and house floor. However, 22.78 per cent cook daily-food. About 16 per cent of them work as baby sitter. Next to them those who supervise agricultural work frequently account for 10.13 per cent or 8 women.

*(v)* In a total number of 25 or in 17.48 per cent of cases, sons become irritated towards their parents when they do not work but comparatively in more cases, i.e., 32 or 22.38 per cent, daughters-in-laws show their dissatisfaction towards their parents-in-law in various ways.

**Social Relationship with Family Members, Renderance of Consultancy Service During Social Crisis and Involvement in the Process of Decision-making**

*(i)* Human beings are social animals. They procreate children for various reasons, viz, to attain parenthood (78.38%) and ensure continuity of family lineally, old-age security (69.59%), fulfilling the ritual requirement (57.43%), to make them educated and employed in order to ensure higher quality of life (33.78%), and to make them able to sustain the dignity of their family. A total number of 32 or 21.62 per cent did not have any motive rather they procreated children out of their natural impulse.

*(ii)* Of those who had an intention of having old-age security from their children, 25.24 per cent or 26 aged opine that their motives are still unfulfilled since the desired goals are not yet satisfied.

*(iii)* That in case of 11.59 per cent or 17 cases, their sons are separated from their parents. The percentage of separation of sons from their parents is more in case of non-pensioners since their income is very meagre or they do not earn any money in ready cash.

*(iv)* That as many as in 72 or 48.65 per cent of cases, at least one son is serving or doing business and staying away from them.

*(v)* A total number of 18 aged persons accounting for 25 per cent opine that their sons staying outside do not visit them and from amongst those sons who regularly visit their parents at village constitute only 26.93 per cent.

*(vi)* So far as the reasons of not visiting aged parents at all or regularly among the sons staying outside are concerned, most of the parents say that it is because of long distance of the place of work of their sons from their respective villages together with their small salary, which does not facilitate regular contact with them. Surprisingly 36.21 per cent or 21 aged persons held their daughters-in-law responsible for this sad happening. However, 31.03 per cent or 18 aged persons opine that it is mainly because of the ideological clash and generation gap between them and their children who stay outside their village.

*(vii)* That 41.22 per cent of aged persons visit their sons who stay outside their village. But amongst them, 45.90 per cent regularly visit them and 19.67 per cent visit occasionally depending upon their mood and necessity. Merely, 4.92 per cent visit on all or most of the festive occasions and the rest 29.51 per cent meet their sons when asked for or during crisis/ requiremer

*(viii)* As to the reasons of not visiting sons at all or regularly, highest percentage, i.e., 57.50 opine that it is because of their old age. Next to them 40 per cent opine that they avoid frequent visit because of shortage of accommodation facility. As many as 35 per cent do not like to be some sort of burden on their sons in cities where the cost of living is higher than village establishments. The other reasons of not visiting sons regularly are ill health (25.83%), ill-treatment of daughters-in-law (14.17%), problem of consumption of narcotics and smokes by self (11.67%), and ill treatment of sons (5.00%).

*(ix)* That of the 72 aged, in 40.28 per cent or 29 cases the sons staying outside village remit money for the maintenance of their aged parents. But surprisingly only 17.24 per cent or 5 of them are found to be regular.

(*x*) That 37.31 per cent or 25 aged men are now heading their families and the rest do not. As regards the factors responsible for this, in case of 45.24 or 19 cases, their sons have taken the authority from their parents by repeated imposition of pressure on their father to hand over the responsibility. But 35.71 per cent or 15 aged persons have voluntarily handed over the responsibility of managing home to their sons because of their old age. However, 19.05 per cent or 8 persons of them are not heading families because of dissatisfaction and frustration in familial life.

(*xi*) In patriarchal societies, even though the male members head their families, the role of females is very important who manage the home. They maintain a superior status over their daughters-in-law by managing home. But only about 37 per cent or 30 of them are now managing home and for the rest of the cases their daughters-in-law have taken over the responsibility. The reasons of not managing home, are disinheritance of the authority by daughters-in-law (43.14%) interference of sons to hand over the responsibility to daughters-in-law (31.37%), frustration in family life (13.73%) and old age (11.76%).

(*xii*) That a total number of 24 aged persons accounting for 16.21 per cent opine that their daughters-in-law consider them as social burden whereas 3 or 2.03 per cent say that their sons also think so. An aged man opines that his spouse thinks that he is a burden on her. On the contrary when as many as 68 or 45.95 per cent say that nobody thinks them as social burden, 52 or 35.14 per cent of them did not give any answer thereby indicating a negative answer.

**Renderance of Consultancy Service During Social Crisis and Involvement in Decision-making**

(*i*) In case of 64.19 per cent or 95 cases, children consult their aged parents during household crises and other difficult situations. In case of the rest 35.81 per cent or 53 aged persons their children do not consult.

*(ii)* That of the total 67 aged men, only 13 or 19.40 per cent are the recognised members of their respective village communities. But only 4 or 30.77 per cent of them actively participate in village meetings. However, from amongst the non-members, 6 or 11.11 per cent also actively participate in such meetings. However, of all the aged men, 10 or 14.93 per cent get themselves involved in those meetings.

*(iii)* Of those who take part in village meetings, only 30 per cent say that their decision is accepted and 40 per cent opine that their opinions are valued only in rare cases. According to the rest 30 per cent, their decisions are accepted at times.

**Food and Narcotic Habits**

*(i)* That a total number of 78 aged persons accounting for 18.92 per cent are vegetarian and the rest 120 or 81.08 per cent are non-vegetarian. But comparatively more (29.63%) aged women are vegetarian than the aged men (5.97%).

*(ii)* The most important food items of the aged persons are found to be milk (30.27%), fish (14.19%), meat/ chicken (10.81%), sweet/snacks (8.78%), mango (6.76%), egg (4.05), cheese (2.70%), etc. A total number of 48 persons accounting for 32.43 per cent do not have any specific favourite food items, because they cannot afford to have them.

*(iii)* As regards the provision of favourite food for the aged, it can be said that, highest percentage get in rare cases and there are only 5.17 per cent or 6 persons who are provided with their favourite food items whenever they desire to consume those. However, 17.24 per cent or 20 of them get it occasionally. They are followed by 12.07 per cent or 14 persons who get it frequently or whenever they want. The rest 17.24 per cent or 20 persons claim that they do not get it at all.

*(iv)* That 31.08 per cent are fully satisfied with the food they are provided with daily. Nearly 49 per cent or 72 persons are partly satisfied and the rest 20.27 per cent or 30 persons point out their dissatisfaction on the food they are provided with.

*(v)* That as many as 110 or 74.32 per cent of aged persons are addicted to different narcotics, like betel (50.91%), tobacco paste or *tamaku* (43.64%), *bidi* (20.0%), *khaini* (4.55%), *Ganja* (3.64%), and alcohol (1.82%).

**Health, Disease and the Process of Treatment**

*(i)* That majority of aged people (60.14%) are quite mobile without the help of anybody. They are followed by those who are fairly mobile without the help of walking-sticks (19.59), fairly mobile with the help of walking-sticks (12.84%), and slightly mobile with the help of a person (4.05%). A total number of 5 persons or 3.38 per cent are immobile or bedridden.

*(ii)* That a total number of 130 aged accounting for 87.84 per cent are suffering from at least one disease.

*(iii)* That highest percentage of aged men suffer from rheumatism (29.03%) but it is weak eye sight (17.65%) in case of aged women.

*(iv)* Irrespective of sex, highest percentage of aged persons suffer from rheumatism. The other important diseases from which these people suffer are weak eye sight (20.00%), high blood pressure (19.23%), constipation (17.69%), asthma (14.62%), cold and cough (10.00%), giddiness (10.00%), gastritis (9.23%), diabetes (8.46%), heart problem (7.69%), loss of speech (6.92%), forgetfulness (6.15%), piles (5.38%), hearing problem (4.62%), waist/back pain (4.62%), urinary problem (3.08%), filaria (3.08%), low blood pressure (2.31%), paralysis (2.31%), colic/peptic ulcer (1.59%), hydrocele (0.77%), and head-parkinsonism (0.77%).

*(v)* Of the total number of 130 patients, i.e., those who are suffering from at least one disease, only 28 or 21.54 per cent are undergoing medical treatment and the rest do not. But out of the total of 62 men, 19 or 30.65 per cent are undergoing treatment, and there are only 9 or 13.24 per cent of aged women who are under treatment.

*(vi)* Of those patients (28) who are undergoing treatment, 20 or 71.43 per cent are under allopathic treatment followed by 5 or 17.86 per cent who are taking homoeopathic medicines, and the rest 3 or 10.71 per cent are under ayurvedic treatment.

*(vii)* That the cost of treatment of sick aged persons is met by themselves (64.29%), self and sons (14.29%), sons (10.71%), spouse (7.14%), and spouse and son (3.57%).

*(viii)* Out of the total of 28 aged persons who are undergoing some medical treatment, only 9 or 32.14 per cent are satisfied with the treatment they are provided with. Those who are partially satisfied constitute 10 or 35.71 per cent and the rest 9 or 32.14 per cent are not satisfied.

**Leisure and Recreational Activities and the Aged**

*(i)* That of the total aged persons, 64 accounting for 43.24 per cent feel loneliness but comparatively more (67.27%) percentage of pensioners feel loneliness than others. It happens because of their retirement from active routine life.

*(ii)* The aged who feel loneliness to a great extent account for 35.95 per cent and for 42.19 per cent of them, the degree of loneliness is rated as moderate. Those who feel loneliness to some extent account for 21.88 per cent.

*(iii)* That a total number of 120 (81.08%) aged have at least one friend with whom they can share their feelings on day-to-day life.

*(iv)* That the most important recreational activity among the aged is found to be playing cards since it is played by 55 or 37.16 per cent of them either regularly or occasionally. The other recreational activities are gossiping/spending time at village tea stall/meeting pandals (31.76%), watching T.V. (23.65%), reading of religious books/scripts (22.30%), listening to religious recitation (17.56%), listening to radio (17.57%) reading newspaper (11.49%), reading of story books/novels (10.81%), playing *pasa* (3.38%), etc. About 17 percentage of them simply sit at home.

**Drawal of Pension and the Aged**

*(i)* That most (78.95%) of the aged draw their pension from the existing treasuries located within the Bhubaneswar city. The rest, however draw it from public sector lead banks depending upon their choices.

*(ii)* Almost all are to undertake much physical strain since their is no arrangement of sitting facility in the premises of the treasuries, from where they draw their pensions.

**Concluding Remarks**

*(i)* With the growth of population, and at the same time, with the spread of industrialisation and urbanisation, many cultural and social values have lost their importance and significance in traditional social structures. And the people are becoming very materialistic since their aspirations for material possession of new amenities in the modern world have phenomenally increased. This has resulted in the migration of people from rural to urban sectors for fulfilling their aspirations of leading an elite life. In that case the aged parents are left behind at villages or for some other reasons the coherence between generations has severely been disturbed and the life in joint family system has been shattered in eco-friendly socio-traditional environment.

*(ii)* In many cases when the aged persons are earning and contributing their income, they are well behave and respected by their family members, particularly sons and daughters-in-law. If they do not earn and contribute their earning, daughters-in-law becomes very harsh and in that case the status of the aged is reduced to a subordinate stage since they are not consulted in any household matter even if they are active and able to render their advice and expertise in important matters. In some cases, they are considered as non-living objects and hence their social existence becomes immaterial.

*(iii)* Where there is more poverty, there is more discrimination but if, in that case the aged are earning they enjoy a superior status than others.

*(iv)* The degree of discrimination is more prominent and hence visible in less educated families than families where the family members are highly educated.

*(v)* Those who reside with their married sons and grandchildren, most often do not get food as per their own choice or interest even if they earn and contribute their earning to the family. In families where grandchildren are there, the aged are to share the available food, particularly milk with them. Hence, in those families they remain underfed.

*(vi)* The aged persons belonging to middle income group have a greater inclination towards their native villages and they like to spend the rest part of their life in their respective villages.

*(vii)* Many of the retired persons occasionally come over to Bhubaneswar city or to some other towns where their son/s is/are settled but do not like to stay long or permanently with them because of the following important reasons:

*(a)* Their attraction towards their own villages;

*(b)* Shortage of room/space in the residential quarters of their son/s;

(*c*) Lack of contemporary friends of equal status in cities/towns;

(*d*) Less scope of spending time in playing cards/ *Pasa* etc.;

(*e*) Ill treatment or indifference of daughters-in-law;

(*f*) High cost of living in cities and the aged parents do not like to be a burden on son/s in that situation.

(*viii*) Upper caste Hindus are more educated than others and most of them are employed in cities in one way or the other. Hence, the probability of the aged staying separately, among higher caste Hindus, is more than the lower caste Hindus.

(*ix*) Generally daughters-in-law are more often harsh towards their aged parents-in-law than the sons. But the social gap between daughters-in-law and mothers-in-law is more than between daughters-in-law and fathers-in-law.

(*x*) Many aged particularly, aged women sacrifice self-interests and like to adjust with the minimum foodstuff, clothing etc., for the well-being of the whole family members.

(*xi*) Most of the aged suffer from various age-based diseases but remain untreated. But amongst the diseased aged persons, there are less number of diseased women than diseased men who are undergoing treatment either because of the fact that the men are mobile and earning or because of the practice of gender discrimination in traditional societies. In many cases, the diseased women prefer to remain untreated and want that the scarce monetary resource to be spent for the betterment of the family members or for the treatment of their husbands in order to gain ritual merit and that is why they sacrifice their self-interest. This trend is more conspicuous where the aged women are tradition-bound.

# Bibliography


Able, Bruce J and Hayslip, Bret, 1986, Locus of Control and Attitude Towards Work and Retirement. *Journal of Psychology,* 120: 479-487.

Asha, C.B. and Subramanian K.A., 1990, "Problems of Elderly Women" *Indian Journal of Community Guidance Services,* 7 (3): 61-7.

Atchley, Robert C., 1972, "The Social Forces in Latter Life: An Introduction to Social Gerontology in D.E. Poplin (ed) *Social Problems,* Belmout: Wadsworth.

Bali Arun P., 1999, *Understanding Graying People of India* (ed), New Delhi: Inter-India Publication.

Benson, Leonard, 1971, *The Family Bond,* New York: Random House.

Bernstein, M.C. and Joan Brodshaug Bernstein, 1988, *Social Security: The System that Works.* New York: Basic Books.

Bharadwaj, M.A., A. Sen and D. Mathur, 1991, Life Satisfaction in Depressed and Non-Depressed Elderly People, *Indian Journal of Community Guidance Service,* 8: 49-55.

Bhatia H.S., 1983, *Aging and Society: A Sociological Study of Retired Public Servants,* Udaipur: Arya's Book Centre.

Binstock, R.H., 1983, "The Aged as Scapegoat" *The Gerontologist* 12: 265-80.

Binstock, R.H and Shanan, E, 1976, *Handbook of Aging and Social Science*. New York: Van Nostrand Reinfold.

Birren, J.E., 1964, *The Psychology of Ageing*, New Jersey, EC: Prentice Hall.

Biswas, S.K., 1985, "Dependency and Family Care of the Aged in Village India: A Case Study" *Journal of Indian Anthropological Society*, 20: 238-57.

——, 1987 (a), *Ageing in Contemporary India*. Calcutta: Indian Anthropological Society.

——, 1987 (b), Dependency and Family Care of the Aged in Village India—A Case Study in Biswas S.K. (ed) *Ageing in Contemporary India*. Calcutta: Indian Anthropological Society.

Biswas, S.K. and T.P. Tripathy, 1990, A Comparative Study of Employment Situation of the Aged" *Man in India* 70 (1): 26-46.

Bohannan, Paul, 1981, "Food of Old People in Centre City Hotels "in Fry. C.L (et.al) *Dimensions: Aging, Culture and Health*. New York: J.F. Bergin Publishers.

Bose, A.B., 1988, "Policies and Programmes for the Aging in India" in Bose and Gangrad (eds) *Aging in India: Problems and Potentialities*. New Delhi: Abhinav Publications.

K.D. Bose, A.B. and Gangrade (eds), 1988, *The Aging in India: Problems and Potentialities*. New Delhi: Abinav Publications.

Bose, A.B., 1988, "Aging in India: Demographic Dimensions" in A.B. Bose and K.D. Gangrad (eds); *The Aging in India: Problems and Potentialities*. New Delhi: Abhinav Publications.

Burgess, E.W., 1954, "Social Relations, Activities and Personal Adjustment". *The American Journal of Sociology*, LIX (49): 352-60.

Burr, J.A. and J.E, Mutchler, 1994, Ethnic Living Arrangements: "Cultural Convergence or Cultural Manifestation?" *Social Forces*. 72: 169-79.

Burus, R.K., 1954, "Economic Aspects of Aging and Retirement". *American Journal of Sociology* LIX (Jan): 384-390.

Calasauti, T.M., 1993, "Bringing Diversity Towards an Inclusive Theory of Retirement". *Journal of Aging Studies* 7: 133-56.

Cary S. Kart, 1981, *The Realities of Aging: An Introduction to Gerontology*. London: Allyn and Bacion, iue.

Chandi Prasad, 1983, *Changing Family Structure and Welfare Needs of the Aged Among Low Income Groups (Project Report)*. Agra University: Institute of Social Science.

Choudhury, D. Paul, 1992, *Aging and the Aged: A Source Book*, New Delhi: Inter-India Publication.

Chauhana, H.B. and P.P. Talwar, 1987, "Aging in India": Its Socio Economic and Health Implications". *Asia-Pacific Population Journal*. 3 (2): 23-38.

Clarke, C.J. and L.J. Neidert, 1992, "Living Arrangements of the Elderly: An Examination of Differences According to Ancestry and Generation". *The Gerontologist* 32: 796-804.

Clark, D. and G. Maddox, 1993, "Race. Aging and Functional Health: Evidence of Selective Survival", *Journal of Aging and Health* 54: 536-57.

Coe, R.M., 1990, "Policy Priorities for Health Care for the Elderly in Developing Countries". *Journal of Kerala Sociology Society* 18 (2): 20-27.

Cohen, Wilbur and Milton Friedra, 1972, *Social Security Universal or Selective?* Washington, DC: American Enterprise Institute.

Coleman, J.W. and Cressey, D.R., 1980, *Social Problems*, New Delhi: Harper and Row.

Crystal, S and D. Shea, 1990, "The Economic Well-being of the Elderly", *Review of Income and Wealth*. 36: 227-47.

Dak, T.M. and Sharma M.L., 1987, "Changing Status of the Old in North Indian Villages, in Sharma, M.L. and Dak T.M. eds. Aging in India. New Delhi: Ajanta Publications.

Dandekar, Kumudini, 1996, *The Elderly in India*. New Delhi: Saga.

Dandekar, K., 1997, "The Aged, Their Problems, Social Intervention and Future Outlook for Maharashtra" in A.S. Kohli (ed), *Social Welfare*, New Delhi: Anmol.

Desai, K.G., 1982, *Aging in India*. Bombay: Tata Institute of Social Sciences.

——, 1985, "Situation of the Aged in India" Journal of *Indian Anthropological Society*: 20 (3) 201-9.

De Souza, Alfred, 1981, *The Social Organisation of Aging Among the Urban Poor*. New Delhi: Indian Social Institute.

De Souza, Alfred and Walter Fernandes, 1982, *Aging in South Asia: Theoretical Issues and Policy Implications*. New Delhi: Indian Social Institute.

Dowd, J.J. and V.L. Bengtson, 1978, "Aging in Minority Populations. An Examination of the Double Jeopardy Hypothesis". *Journal of Gerontology* 33: 427-36.

Dutt, S.K., 1986, "Aging and Nutrition. *The Hindustan Times*. September 27, p. 8.

Fisher, D.H., 1978, *Growing Old in America*. Oxford, UK. Oxford University Press.

Fry G.L. et.al, 1981, *Dimensions: Aging, Culture and Health*. New York: J.F. Bergin Publishers.

Gaag, JV ed and Alexander Preker, 1998, "Health Care for Aging Populations: Issues and Options" in Prescott Nicholas. *Choices in Financing Health Care and Old Age Security*. World Bank Discussion Paper No. 392. Washington DC: The World Bank.

Gangrade, K.J., 1988, Crisis of Values: A Sociological Study of the Old and the Young" in Bose A.B. and Gangrade, K.D (eds). *The Aging in India: Problems and Potentialities*. New Delhi: Abhinav Publications.

——, 1989, "Emerging Conception at Aging in India". *Eastern Anthropologist* 42 (2): 151-69.

Glascock, A.P. and S.L. Feinman, 1981, "Social Asset or Social Burden: Treatment of the Aged in Non-Industrial Societies" in Fry, G.L. et.al *Dimensions: Aging, Culture and Health,* New York: J.F. Bergain Publishers.

G.O.I., 1951, *Census of India,* Paper No. 3, 1954, Age Tables—1951.

——, 1961, *Census of India,* 1961, Vol. I, Part-II (i), Social and Cultural Tables.

——, 1961, *Census of India,* 1961, Vol. XII, Orissa, Part-II-A, General Population Tables.

——, 1961, *Census of India,* 1961, Vol. I, Part-II A (ii), Union Primary Census Abstracts.

——, 1961, *Census of India,* 1971, Series—I, Part-II-C (ii) Social and Cultural Tables.

——, 1961, *Census of India,* Paper No. 2 of 1963, Age Tables.

——, 1971, *Census of India,* 1971, Series-I, Part-II-C (ii) Social and Cultural Tables.

——, 1991, *Census of India,* Part-II-A (i), General Tables A-1 to A-3.

——, 1991, *Census of India,* 1991, Series-I, Final Population Tables: Brief analysis of Primary Census Abstract, Paper-2 of 1992.

——, 1991, *Village Primary Census Abstract,* Bhubaneswar Block (unpublished).

Gore, M.S., 1998, *Urbanisation and Family Change*. Bombay: Popular Prakashan.

——, 1988, "Family Support to Elderly People: The Indian Situation", WHO Monograph. *Family Support to Elderly People, The International Experience,* p. 22.

——, 1992, "Aging of the Human Being", *The Indian Journal of Social Work,* L III (2): 212-219.

Guha Roy, S., 1991, "Perspective on the Population Aging in India" in Indira J. Prakash (ed). *Quality Aging,* Varanasi: BHU.

Gurumurthy, K.G., 1998, *The Aged in India*. New Delhi: Reliance Publishing House.

——, 1978, 'Rural Aged' (Grameena Vruddaru). *Manavika Bharati*: 2 (2): 78-85.

Haber, Carole and Brian Gratton, 1994, *Old Age and the Search for Security: An American Social History*. Bloomington: Indiana University.

Habar, B.G., 1989, "Aging in India: An Anthropological Perspective", in Nair and Ramana (eds) *Aging and Welfare of the Elderly in India*. Madras: Madras Institute of Aging.

Handler, P., 1960, "Radiation and Aging" in N.W. Shock (ed), *Aging*, Washington D.C.: American Association for the Advancement of Science.

Hareven, T.K. and K.J. Admas (eds), 1982, *Aging Life and Course Transitions—An Interdisciplinary Perspective*, London: Tavistock.

Haugh, M.R., 1989, "Coping Resources and Selective Survival in Mental Health and Elderly", *Research on Aging*. 11: 468-9.

Herman, J. Leother, 1967, *Problems of Aging*. California: Dickenson Publishing Company.

Hess, B.B., 1976, "Introduction" in B.B. Hess (ed), *Growing Old in America*, New Jersey: Transaction Books.

Husain, M.G. (ed), 1997, *Changing Indian Society and Status of Aged*. New Delhi: Manak Publications (P) Ltd.

ICMR, 1984, *Task Force Project on Problems of the Aged Seeking Psychiatric Help*. New Delhi: ICMR.

Indian Statistical Institute. (Demographic Research Unit)., 1986, *Reconstruction of Indian Life Tables for 1901-81 and Projections for 1981-2000*. Calcutta: Indian Statistical Institute.

International Labour Office, 1989, *The Last of Social Security*. Geneva, Switzerland: ILO.

Irudya Rajan, S., 1989, "Aging in Kerala: One Move Population Problems?" *Asia Pacific Population Journal* 4 (2): 46.

Iswaran, K., 1986, "Interdependence of the Elementary and Expanded Family" in Augustine, J.N. (ed). New Delhi: Vikas Publishing House.

Jagannathan, V., and C.M. Palvia, 1978, *Problems of Pensioners: Socio-economic Policy and Administration*. Delhi: Lalit Prakashan.

James E. Birren, 1959, *Handbook of Aging and the Individual*. Chicago: The University of Chicago.

Jarry, D and J. Jarry, 1995, *Collins Dictionary of Sociology*. Glassgow: Collins Publishers.

Jerry Jacobs, 1974, *Fun City: An Ethnographic Study of a Retirement Community*. New York Inc: Holt, Rinehart and Winston.

Jitendra Prasad, 1987, "Perspective on Aging" Sharma M.L. and T.M. Dak (eds) *Aging in India: Challenge for the Society*, Delhi: Ajanta Publications.

Joha B, Willianson, Anne, Munley and Linda, Evans, 1980, *Aging and Society: An Introduction to Social Gerontology*. New York: Hold, Rinehart and Winstron.

Joseph, Johi C., 1988, "Interaction Between the Old and the Young" *Social Welfare*, 35 (6): 17-23.

Joesph, J., 1991, *Aged in India—Problems and Personality*, Allahabad: Chugh.

Khan, M.Z., 1997, "Voluntary Welfare Services for the Aged", in A.S. Kohli (ed) *Social Welfare*, New Delhi: Anmol.

Kingson, Eric and Edward, D. Berkowitz, 1993, *Social Secularity and Medicare: A Policy Primer.* Westport, CT: Auburn House.

Kohili, A.S, 1996, *Social Situation of the Aged in India*. New Delhi: Anmol Publications Pvt. Ltd.

Koyano, W., 1989, "Japanese Attitudes Toward the Elderly: A Review of Research Findings". *Journal of Cross-Cultural Gerontology*, 4: 325-45.

Kumar Reddy, J.S. and Ramamurti, P.V., 1990, "Stress and Coping Strategies of the Rural Aged" *Journal of Personality and Clinical Studies*, 6: 171-6.

Kumar, S.V., 1991, *Family Life and Socio-Economic Problems of the Aged*. New Delhi: Ashish Publishing House.

Kuypers, J.A., 1972, "Changeability of Life Style and Personality in Old Age". *Gerontologist*, 12: 336-347.

Lakhminarayan, T.R., and Malathi, G. 1991, 1991, "Campaign of Lonely Aged and Aged Couples—A Study in Rural Settings" *The Minds* 18: 1-4.

Laslett, Peter, 1991, A Fresh Map of Life: The Emergence of the Third Age, Cambridge, MA: Harvard University Press.

Lumpkin, J.R., 1986, "The Relationship Between Locus of Control and Age—New Evidence", *Journal of Social Behaviours and Personality*, 1 (2): 245-252.

Margaret Hellie Huyek, 1974, *Growing Older*. London: Prentice Hall International.

Marulasiddaiah, H.M., 1969, *Old People of Makunti*. Dharwad: Karnataka University.

Mishra Saraswati, 1987, *Social Adjustment in Old Age*. New Delhi: B.R. Publishing House.

——, 1989, *Problems and Social Adjustment in Old Age: A Sociological Analysis*. New Delhi: Gian Publishing House.

Mohanty, S., 1989, "Retired Govt. Servants and Problems of Socio-Psychological Adjustment" in R.N. Pati and B. Jena (eds), *Aged in India*. New Delhi: Ashish Publishing House.

Mukharjee, B.M., 1997, "The Aged: Their Problems, Social Intervention and Future Outlooks in Madhya Pradesh" in A.S. Kohli (ed) *Social Welfare*. New Delhi: Anmol.

Muthaya, B.C., and M. Aneesuddin, 1997, "Rural Aged: Existing Conditions, Problems and Possible Interventions (A Study in Andhra Pradesh)", in A.S. Kohli, *Social Welfare*. New Delhi: Anmol.

Muttagi, P.K., 1997, *Aging Issues and Old Age Care*. New Delhi: Classical Publishing Company.

Nag, N.G., 1987, "Welfare Services for the Aged", *Encyclopaedia of Social Work in India*, 3: 344-353.

Nageshwar, H.V., 1992, "The Problems and the Care of the Aged in India", in J. Sarkar (ed), *Social Problems and Welfare in India*. New Delhi: A.P.H.

Nagpal, Nishi, 1991, "Social Support and Life Satisfaction Among Aged" *Indian Journal of Psychometry and Education*. 22 (2): 91-11.

Neogarten, B.L., 1980, "Aged Norms, Age Constraints, and Adult Socialisation", in J.S. Quadagro (ed), *Aging, the Individual and Society—Readings in Social Gerontology*. New York: St. Martin's Press.

Neogarten, Dial A, ed., 1996, *The Meaning of Age: Selected Prepares of Bernice L. Neugarten*. Chicago: University of Chicago Press.

Nydegger, C.N., 1981, "Gerontology and Anthropology, Challenge and Opportunity" in Fry, G.L. et. al (eds) *Dimensions: Aging, Culture and Health*, New York: J.F. Bergin Publishers.

Orenstein, H., 1961, "The Recent History of the Extended Family in India". *Social Problems*, 8 (2) 341-50.

Palmore Erdman and Kenneth Mauton, 1961, Modernisation and the Status of the Aged: International Comparisons", *Journal of Gerontology*, 29 (2): 205-210.

Pampel, F.C., and M Hardy, 1994, "Changes in Income Inequality During Old Age", *Research in Stratification and Mobility*, 13: 239-64.

——, 1994, "Status Maintenance and Change During Old Age", *Social Forces*, 73: 289-314.

Pampel, F.C., 1998, *Aging, Social Inequality, and Public Policy*. California: Pine Forge Press.

Pasnicha, S., and B.V.S Thimayamma, 1997, *Dietary Tips for the Elderly*. Hyderabad: National Institute of Nutrition.

Pati, R.N. and B. Jena (ed)., 1989, Problems of the Aged in India, New Delhi: Asish Publishing House.

Pathak, J.D., 1980, *Our Elderly*. Bombay: Tata Institute of Social Science.

Poplin, D.E. (ed)., 1979, *Social Problems*. London: Foresman and Co.

Prescott, Nicholas, 1998, *Choices in Financing Health Care and Old Age Security, World Bank Discussion Paper No. 392*. 1997. Washington D.C. The World Bank.

Quadagno Jill S., 1998, *Aging, the Individual and Society-Readings in Social Gerontology*. New York: St. Martins Press.

Quinu, J.F., 1987, "The Economic Status of the Elderly: Beware of the Mean", *Review of Income and Wealth*. 33: 63-82.

Raja, D.A.P., 1997, "The Aged: Their Problems, Social Intervention and Future Outlook in the State of Tamil Nadu", in A.S. Kohli, *Social Welfare*, New Delhi: Anmol.

Rajeswar Prasad, "Reflections on this Problems of Aged in India", *International Journal of Social Research*. XXXIII (4): 387-391.

Ramachandran, Vetal, 1981, "Family Structure and Mental Illness in Old Age", *Indian Journal of Psychiatry* 23: 21-26.

Ramamurti, P.V. and D. Jamuna, 1984, "Psychological Research on the Aged in India", *Journal of Anthropological Society of India*, 19 (3): 269-286.

Rao, K.S., 1994, *Aging*. New Delhi: National Book Trust.

Rejda, George E., 1994, *Social Insurance and Economic Security 5th ed*. Englewood Cliffs, NJ: Prentice Hall.

Riley, M.W and Foner, A., 1968, Parish Clergy and the Aged: Examining Sterotypes, *Journal of Gerontology*, 3dl (3): 340-345.

Ron Avira, 1998, "Social Security Financing Policies and Rapidly Aging Populations" in Presco H, Nicholas *Choices in Financing Health Care and Old Age Security, World Bank Discussion Paper No. 392*. 1997. Washington D.C. The World Bank.

Sahayam, M. Deva, 1988, 'Aged Female: The Most Deprived Among the Deprived", Indian Journal of Social Work XLIX (3): 261-269.

Santhakumari, R., 1992 *The Aging, Their Problems and Need For Social Interaction*. Trivandrum: Centre for Social Research.

Sati, P.N., 1997, "A Study of Aged, Their Problems and Need for Social Intervention (Rajastan)" A.S. Kohili (ed), *Social Welfare*, New Delhi: Anmol.

Sengupta, D.K. and A.K. Chakraborty, "Health Status of Aged 55 Years and Above in Slum Area of Calcutta" *Indian Journal of Public Health,* 26 (2): 112-117.

Schuiz, J.H, 1992, "Economic Security in Old Age: The Role of Social Insurance in Developing Countries" *International Social Security Review* 4: 7599.

Shaben, Ara, 1994, *Old Age Among Slum Dwellers*. New Delhi: South Asian Publishers.

Sharma, M.L and Dak, T.M eds., 1987, *Aging in India, Challenge for the Society*. Delhi: Ajanta Publications.

Sheldon, H.D., 1958, *The Older Population of the United States*. New York: John Wiley and Sons.

Singh Banvir, 1989, "The Aged in Peasantry: Their Socio-economic and Other Problems" *Journal of Social Research,* 3233 (1-2): 131-134.

Sinha, A.C., 1997, "Senior Citizens of Meghalaya: A Study of Problems of the Aged and Need for Social Intervention" in A.S. Kohli (ed), *Social Welfare,* New Delhi: Anmol.

Social Security Administration, 1985, *Social Security Throughout the World,* Washington D.C: U.S. Govt. Printing Office.

Soodan, K.S., 1997, *Aging in India.* Calcutta: Minerva Associates and Publications.

Srivastav, R.C., 1994, *The Problems of the Aged*. New Delhi: Classical Publications.

Stab, Holdger, R., 1982, *Social Consequences of Long Life*. Springfield: C.C. Thomas.

The Samaj, 1998, "Bharatiyamananka Harahari Paramayu Athasathi Varsa—Budhabudhi Mananka Varanaposona Pain Jatiyastaraara Asian Heba", in *The Samaj,* (in Oriya), 6.4.1998. Cuttack: Lokasevak Mandal.

Tibbitts, C., 1960, "Aging as a Model Social Achievement" in C. Tibbitts and W. Donahue (eds), *Aging in Today's Society*. New Jersey: Prentico Hall.

Townsend, Peter, 1987, *The Family Life of Old People*. London: Roultedge and Kegan Paul.

UNESCO, 1982, *Special Issue for World Assembly on Aging*, Paris: UNESCO Press.

United Nations, 1956, *The Aging of Populations and its Economic and Social Implications*. Dept. of Economic and Social Affairs. New York: UN.

——, 1983, *Vienna International Plan of Action on Aging*. New York: UN.

——, 1988, *Economic and Social Implications of Population Aging*. Proceedings of the International Symposium on Population Structure and Development, Tokyo. New York: UN.

Usha Rani, D., Rajaseskharan M. and Naidu D.A., 1987, "Old Age Security and Utility of Children" in Pati, R.N. and Jena, B. eds. *Aged in India*. New Delhi: Ashish Publishing House.

Venkaba Rao, A., 1987, *Problems of the Aged Seeking Psychiatric Help*. National Task Force Project. New Delhi: ICMR.

——, 1988, *India's Grey Sector*. Annals of National Academy of Medical Sciences, 25: 63-7.

——, 1990, *Health Care of Rural Aged*. New Delhi: Indian Council of Medical Research.

Vermani, Savita and Sharma, M.L., 1987, "Younger People's Perception of the Aged", in Sharma, M.L. and Dak T.M. eds. *Aging in India*. New Delhi: Ajanta Publications.

Vijay Kumar, S., 1991, *Family Life and Socio-Economic Problems of the Aged*. New Delhi: Ashish.

Ward, R.A., 1979, The Aging Experience, New York: J.B. Lippincott Co.

Wechler, D., 1955, "The Measurement and Evaluation of Intelligence of Older Persons" in E. Edinburg and S. Living Stone (eds) *Old Age*.

W.H.O., 1982, *Recommendations of the World Health Organisation Conference on Aging*. New Delhi: W.H.O.

# Appendix—1

**NABAKRUSHNA CHOUDHURY CENTRE FOR DEVELOPMENT STUDIES, ORISSA, BHUBANESWAR**

"Problems of the Aged in Oriya Middle Class Caste Hindu Families in Some Selected Fringe Villages of Bhubaneswar city".

(Please put '✓' mark wherever applicable)

1. Name:
2. Age:
3. Sex:
4. Caste:
5. Sub-caste:
6. Present Address:
7. Block:
8. District:
9. Total number of children you have

| *Sl. No.* | *Children* | *Sex* | *Education* | *Marital status* | | | *Occupation* | *Residence within village/ near-by* | *Far-away* |
|---|---|---|---|---|---|---|---|---|---|
| | | | | *M* | *UM* | *W* | | | |
| *(1)* | *(2)* | *(3)* | *(4)* | *(5)* | *(6)* | *(7)* | *(8)* | *(9)* | *(10).* |
| *1st* | | | | | | | | | |
| *2nd* | | | | | | | | | |

*(Contd...)*

| |
|---|
| 3rd |
| 4th |
| 5th |
| 6th |

10. Family background with whom you are presently staying:

| Sl. No. | Name | Age | Sex | Relationship with you | Marital status | Education | Occupation |
|---|---|---|---|---|---|---|---|
| (1) | (2) | (3) | (4) | (5) | (6) | (7) | (8) |
| 1. | | | | | | | |
| 2. | | | | | | | |
| 3. | | | | | | | |
| 4. | | | | | | | |
| 5. | | | | | | | |
| 6. | | | | | | | |
| 7. | | | | | | | |
| 8. | | | | | | | |
| 9. | | | | | | | |
| 10. | | | | | | | |

11. Household Income:

| Sl. No. | Source | Income | Remark |
|---|---|---|---|
| (1) | (2) | (3) | (4) |
| 1. | Salary of your sons | | |
| 2. | Salary of your daughters | | |
| 3. | Your pension | | |
| 4. | Interest of bank balance | | |
| 5. | Rental house/movable assets | | |
| 6. | Agriculture | | |
| 7. | Part time job of yourself/others | | |
| 8. | Livestock | | |

12. Your personal service background:

| *Sl. No.* | *State Govt./ Central Govt.* | *Dept.* | *Last post held* | *Retirement age* | *Last salary drawn* | *Pension* |
|---|---|---|---|---|---|---|
| (1) | (2) | (3) | (4) | (5) | (6) | (7) |
| 1. | State Govt./ Central Govt. | | | | | |
| 2. | Semi Govt. | | | | | |
| 3. | Autonomous | | | | | |
| 4. | Non-Govt. | | | | | |

13. Social responsibility towards children and expectation from them.

    *(a)* You/your spouse have spent quite a good amount of money on the education of your children but what were your expectations from them?

| *Sl. No.* | *Expectations* | *Son* | *Daughter* | *Expectation fulfilled or not Yes/No* |
|---|---|---|---|---|
| (1) | (2) | (3) | (4) | (5) |
| 1. | Old-age security/ insurance | | | |
| 2. | To take them educated employed | | | |
| 3. | To make them to sustain the family dignity | | | |
| 4. | Any other, please specify | | | |

14. Living arrangement:

    (a) Do you have any other married sons? *Yes/No.*
    If yes, where do they stay now?

    *(i)* In the same village

    *(ii)* At the place of their occupation/job

    *(b)* If they stay in the same village/other places why do not you stay with them?

    *(i)* because of bitter relationship with them

    *(ii)* because of the rotational arrangement

- *(iii)* because of more likeness to the son with whom you are now staying
- *(iv)* because of your love to your village
- *(v)* they do not like to keep you with them.

*(c)* How many rooms are there of your son with whom you are staying now?

*(d)* Do you think that are these sufficient for all the members to stay comfortably? *Yes/No*

*(e)* If yes, do you have a separate room for personal use? If no, where do you stay? *Yes/No*

- *(i)* On the venandah
- *(ii)* At any room depending upon the situation and as per the instructional/arrangement made by daughter-in-law son/spouse/etc.
- *(iii)* In a room of some other person of the village
- *(iv)* Club house/any other (please specify).

*(f)* Do you feel loneliness? *Yes/No*
If yes,

- *(i)* highly isolated
- *(ii)* moderately isolated
- *(iii)* least isolated

*(g)* If you stay alone or with a son, do you get remittance from other sons who are staying outside? *Yes/No.*

- *(i)* If yes,
  - *(a)* Regularly
  - *(b)* Irregularly
  - *(c)* Occasionally
  - *(d)* As and when necessary
- *(ii)* Is the remittance you get from them is enough for you? *Yes/No*

*(h)* Do they visit you? *Yes/No*
If yes,

*(i)* Regularly

*(ii)* Irregularly

*(iii)* Occasionally

*(iv)* Only when you ask them

*(v)* Only when you fall ill

*(vi)* Only during crisis

*(vii)* Whenever they like so

If they do not visit you then why?

(1)

(2)

(3)

(4)

*(i)* Do you visit them? *Yes/No*
If yes,

*(i)* Regularly

*(ii)* Irregularly

*(iii)* Occasionally

*(iv)* Only when they ask you

*(v)* Only when they fall ill

*(vi)* Only during crisis

*(vii)* Whenever you like so

If you do not visit them, then why?

(1)

(2)

(3)

(4)

*(j)* Do not you feel that you should enjoy their company, particularly, grandchildren? *Yes/No*
If no, why?

*(k)* Do the family members of your son with whom you are now staying have good relationship with all the neighbours? *Yes/No*

If no, are you restricted to talk with those neighbours? If yes, why? *Yes/No*

*(l)* What are the topics you generally discuss with your neighbour-friends?

*(i)* Religion

*(ii)* National/State Politics

*(iii)* Village politics

*(iv)* Health of self

*(v)* Negligence on medical treatment

*(vi)* Grandchildren

*(vii)* Ill treatment of sons

*(viii)* Ill treatment of daughter-in-law

*(ix)* Donation of your properly to charitable/religious institutions.

15. Economic predicament/contribution *Ways of Expenditure*

| *Income source* | *Occupancy right* | *Appx. income earned per month/ annum* | *Gives to the son with whom you stay* | *It is divided among all sons* | *I use it for my personal purpose* | *Any other* |
|---|---|---|---|---|---|---|
| (1) | (2) | (3) | (4) | (5) | (6) | (7) |
| Retired pensioner | | | | | | |
| Total land holding | | | | | | |
| Others (Tree/ cattle/goats/etc.) | | | | | | |

16. Decision-making in family and in the community.

(*a*) Are you now heading your family? *Yes/No*

If yes, why.

(*i*)

(*ii*)

(*iii*)

If no, why

(*i*)

(*ii*)

(*iii*)

(*b*) Areas of decision-making at household level

| *Sl. No.* | *Areas of decision* | *Solved by self* | *In consultation with son/others* |
|---|---|---|---|
| *(1)* | *(2)* | *(3)* | *(4)* |
| 1. | Household expenditure | | |
| 2. | Attending social functions of village | | |
| 3. | Attending social function at relatives house | | |
| 4. | Agricultural development | | |
| 5. | Contribution of physical labour/economic assistance for village functions | | |
| 6. | Your personal movement/ visiting other places | | |
| 7. | Your staying arrangement with son/s | | |
| 8. | Your staying arrangement alone at village | | |
| 9. | Marriage ceremony of your son/daughter | | |
| 10. | Thread ceremony of your grandson | | |
| 11. | Marriage ceremony of your grandson | | |
| 12. | Selling of landed or other properties | | |
| 13. | Any other property (please specify) | | |

(c) Decision-making at community level.

(i) Are you a member of your village community? Yes/No

(ii) If yes, are you invited to participate in all the village, meetings? Yes/No

(iii) If yes, do you participate in decision-making? Yes/No

(iv) If yes, whether your decision is accepted by all the members? Yes/No

If Yes,

| Variables | Your generation | Younger generation |
|---|---|---|
| (1) | (2) | (3) |
| Most of the times | | |
| Sometimes | | |
| In rare cases | | |

17.

(v) If the people of younger generation do not accept your decision, then why?

(a) Work participation/contribution of physical labour

| Sl. No. | Work/Activities | Frequent (F) Occasionally (O) Not at all (N) | Out of compulsion | | | Out of own interest | | |
|---|---|---|---|---|---|---|---|---|
| | | | F | O | N | F | O | N |
| (1) | (2) | (3) | (4) | (5) | (6) | (7) | (8) | |
| 1. | Going for shopping | | | | | | | |
| 2. | Supervision of agricultural operation | | | | | | | |
| 3. | Looking after infantile grandchildren | | | | | | | |
| 4. | Visiting relatives | | | | | | | |
| 5. | Any other (please specify) | | | | | | | |

(*b*) If you cannot perform the above activities what are the consequences?

18. (*a*) Leisure and recreational activities

| *Sl. No.* | *Activities* | *Availability Yes/No* | *Interested, Yes/No* | *If Yes* | | | |
|---|---|---|---|---|---|---|---|
| | | | | *Regularly* | *Irregularly* | *Occasionally* | *Rarely* |
| (1) | (2) | (3) | (4) | (5) | (6) | (7) | (8) |
| 1. | Religious readings/listening at village meeting pandal | | | | | | |
| 2. | Other readings (story books, novels etc.) | | | | | | |
| 3. | Newspaper | | | | | | |
| 4. | Listening to Radio | | | | | | |
| 5. | Watching T.V. | | | | | | |
| 6. | Viewing movies in cinema halls | | | | | | |
| 7. | Morning walk | | | | | | |
| 8. | Gossiping/spending time at village tea stall/meeting pandal | | | | | | |
| 9. | Playing cards/other games | | | | | | |
| 10. | Simply sitting alone | | | | | | |
| 11. | Organising village festivals (*Asthaprahari*, *Ramlila* etc.) | | | | | | |
| 12. | Going on pilgrimage | | | | | | |

(*b*) If you play cards, please specify the time.

(*c*) If you play it at night and return late to home, how do your family members react?

(*i*) Son becomes irritant. *Yes/No*

(*ii*) Daughter-in-law becomes indifferent. *Yes/No*

(*iii*) Any other please specify.

19. Social relationship with family members

| | | | *Nature* | | | *Your relationship with them* | | | | | | | | |
|---|---|---|---|---|---|---|---|---|---|---|---|---|---|---|
| *Sl. No.* | *Name* | *Relationship with you* | *Irrespon-sible* | *Indisci-plined* | *Selfish* | *Dis-obedient* | *Cordial* | *Normal* | *Non-cordial* | *No relation-ship* | *Whether they obey you? Yes/ No* | *If yes, out of Respect (R) Fear (F) Griva-nce (G) Pity (P)* | *Whom do you like most and least* | *Why* |
| *(1)* | *(2)* | *(3)* | *(4)* | *(5)* | *(6)* | *(7)* | *(8)* | *(9)* | *(10)* | *(11)* | *(12)* | *(13)* | *(14)* | *(15)* |
| 1. | | | | | | | | | | | | | | |
| 2. | | | | | | | | | | | | | | |
| 3. | | | | | | | | | | | | | | |
| 4. | | | | | | | | | | | | | | |
| 5. | | | | | | | | | | | | | | |
| 6. | | | | | | | | | | | | | | |
| 7. | | | | | | | | | | | | | | |
| 8. | | | | | | | | | | | | | | |
| 9. | | | | | | | | | | | | | | |
| 10. | | | | | | | | | | | | | | |
| 11. | | | | | | | | | | | | | | |
| 12. | | | | | | | | | | | | | | |

20. Health, disease, physical mobility and treatment system

    *(a)* Name of the major diseases you are now suffering from

    *(i)* Asthma

    *(ii)* Blood pressure

    *(iii)* Blindness

    *(iv)* Cold and cough

    *(v)* Constipation

    *(vi)* Diabetes

    *(vii)* Gastric

    *(viii)* Hearing problem

    *(ix)* Loss of speech (full/partly)

    *(x)* Paralysis

    *(xi)* Piles

    *(xii)* Rheumatism

    *(xiii)* Tuberculosis

    *(xiv)* Urinary problem

    *(xv)* Giddiness

    *(xvi)* Heart problem

    *(xvii)* Any other, please specify

    *(b)* What are the treatment going on for improving your health condition?

    *(i)* Continuation of medicine in consultation with the doctor

    *(ii)* Continuation of medicine in consultation with the chemist/medicine sales men

    *(iii)* Continuation of medicine in consultation with the local health-worker/quack

    *(iv)* Continuation of traditional medicine in consultation with the local traditional medicine man

- *(v)* Continuation of traditional herbal medicine in consultation with the traditional healer/shaman.
- *(vi)* No treatment.

*(c)* Who bears the cost of the consultation fee with the doctor and medicine?

- *(i)* Yourself
- *(ii)* Son with whom you are presently staying
- *(iii)* Son with whom you are not staying
- *(iv)* Out of the family-fund of all son/s
- *(v)* Your money plus the money of your sons
- *(vi)* Grandchildren
- *(vii)* Any other means (please specify)

*(d)* If your son bears the cost whether he or any of his family members is irritated/hesitated to spend money on your health? *Yes/No*

If yes, who are they

- *(i)* Son
- *(ii)* Son's wife
- *(iii)* Son's son (please specify the number)
- *(iv)* Son's daughter (please specify the number)
- *(v)* Spouse
- *(vi)* Daughter
- *(vii)* Any other (please specify)

*(e)* Are you satisfied with the treatment going on for improving your health condition? *Yes/No*

If yes,

- *(i)* highly satisfied
- *(ii)* moderately satisfied
- *(iii)* least satisfied
- *(iv)* if not satisfied, then why

(*f*) Are you now mobile? *Yes/No*

If yes

(*i*) Quite mobile

(*ii*) Fairly mobile

(*iii*) Slightly mobile

(*iv*) Mobile with the help of a walking-stick

(*v*) Bedridden

(*vi*) If no, why?

(*g*) Are you now able to

| *Sl. No.* | *Variables* | *Yes/ No* | *If no, who helps* | *Regularly (R) Irregularly (I) Occasionally (O)* | *Spontaneously* | *with reluctance* |
|---|---|---|---|---|---|---|
| (1) | (2) | (3) | (4) | (5) | (6) | (7) |
| 1. | Clean your teeth | | | | | |
| 2. | Going to latrine | | | | | |
| 3. | Pass urine | | | | | |
| 4. | Taking bath | | | | | |
| 5. | Eating | | | | | |
| 6. | Self-dressing | | | | | |
| 7. | Walking on road | | | | | |
| 8. | Washing clothes | | | | | |

(*h*) Do they think that you are a burden on them? *Yes/No*

If yes who are they and why?

(*i*) Son

(*ii*) Son's wife

(*iii*) Son's son

(*iv*) Son's daughter

(*v*) Any other (please specify)

(i) Your daily diet

| Variables | Items (please specify) |
| --- | --- |
| Morning lightfood | |
| Mid-day meal | |
| Afternoon snacks | |
| Late evening food | |

(j) Are you satisfied with the items provided to you?

If no, why? *Yes/No*

(k) Do you think that you are being neglected in your nutritional intake? *Yes/No*

If yes why?

(l) Your favourite food items? (please specify)

*(i)*

*(ii)*

*(iii)*

*(iv)*

(m) Are these provided as per your want? *Yes/No*

if yes.

*(i)* Whenever you want

*(ii)* Most frequently

*(iii)* Frequently

*(iv)* Occasionally

*(v)* Rarely

*(vi)* Not at all

If no, why

(n) Do you get sick-food as per the requirement and your need? *Yes/No*

21. (a) Narcotic habits and the reaction of the family members

| Sl. No. | Items | Since when addicted | Are you restricted Yes/No | If yes, who restricts? |
|---|---|---|---|---|
| (1) | (2) | (3) | (4) | (5) |
| 1. | Alcohol | | | |
| 2. | *Bidi* | | | |
| 3. | Cigarette | | | |
| 4. | *Ganja/Bhang* | | | |
| 5. | *Khaini/Dokta* | | | |
| 6. | *Pan* | | | |
| 7. | *Tamaku* (Tobacco) | | | |
| 8. | Opium | | | |
| 9. | Any other (please specify) | | | |

*(b)* Are you io confront with them who restrict you to consume any of the above narcotics? *Yes/No*

If yes,

*(i)* Frequently

*(ii)* Occasionally

*(iii)* Rarely

*(c)* What are the factors responsible for this?

*(i)* It smells bad to them

*(ii)* Creates unclean environment

*(iii)* They are more concerned to your health

*(iv)* It creates an adverse impact on the children

*(v)* They fear that they are to spend more money on your health if you take it but they are not concerned what happens to your health.

22. Your conception towards 'old age' (whom do you consider as an old).

23. Please mention the merit and demerit between the past (your generation) and present (generation of your son) social order (i.e. joint family system)

24. Please specify your major problems

    *(a)*

    *(b)*

    *(c)*

    *(d)*

    *(e)*

25. Your suggestions for your comfort and peace/betterment of the aged people.

    *(a)*

    *(b)*

    *(c)*

    *(d)*

26. Do you think that you have performed your duties to the best satisfaction of your parents? *Yes/No*

    If no, why?

# Appendix—2

## POPULATION PROFILE OF STUDY VILLAGES

| *Sl. No.* | *Name of the village* | *Block* | *Total HHs* | *SC* | *ST* | *Others* | *Total* |
|---|---|---|---|---|---|---|---|
| *(1)* | *(2)* | *(3)* | *(4)* | *(5)* | *(6)* | *(7)* | *(8)* |
| 1. | Balianta | Balianta | 483 | 30.77 (877) | – | 69.23 (1973) | 100.00 (2850) |
| 2. | Satyabhamapur | – | 103 | 64.48 (374) | – | 35.52 (206) | 100.00 (580) |
| 3. | Bhubanpur | – | 616 | 30.26 (821) | 44.93 (1219) | 24.81 (673) | 100.00 (2713) |
| 4. | Gotalagram | – | 142 | 33.52 (298) | – | 66.48 (591) | 100.00 (889) |
| 5. | G. Srirampur | – | 89 | 30.49 (182) | 0.34 (2) | 69.51 (415) | 100.00 (597) |
| 6. | Andilo | – | 291 | 40.26 (742) | – | 59.74 (1101) | 100.00 1843 |
| 7. | Tankapani | – | NA | – | – | – | – |
| 8. | Bhainchua | – | 542 | 5.76 (202) | – | 94.24 (3307) | 100.00 (3509) |
| 9. | Kantunia | – | NA | – | – | – | – |
| 10. | Rahadamunda | – | NA | – | – | – | – |
| 11. | Jasuapur | – | 138 | 27.63 (210) | – | 72.37 (550) | 100.00 (760) |
| 12. | Indrapal | – | 154 | 26.77 (219) | – | 73.23 (599) | 100.00 (818) |

*(Contd...)*

| (1) | (2) | (3) | (4) | (5) | (6) | (7) | (8) |
|---|---|---|---|---|---|---|---|
| 13. | Bikipur | Bhubaneswar | 48 | 9.69<br>(28) | –<br>(261) | 90.31<br>(289) | 100.00 |
| 14. | Itipur | – | 56 | 20.44<br>(65) | –<br>(253) | 79.56<br>(318) | 100.00 |
| 15. | Jaipur | – | 45 | 16.54<br>(43) | – | 83.46<br>(217) | 100.00<br>(260) |
| 16. | Nathapur | – | 310 | 18.44<br>(352) | 0.10<br>(2) | 81.46<br>(1555) | 100.00<br>(1909) |
| 17. | Raghunathpur | – | 454 | 24.53<br>(629) | 6.20<br>(159) | 69.27<br>(1776) | 100.00<br>(2564) |
| 18. | Daruthenga | – | 551 | 15.60<br>(445) | –<br>– | 84.40<br>(2407) | 100.00<br>(2852) |
| 19. | Samodarpur | – | 24 | 18.67<br>(28) | – | 81.33<br>(122) | 100.00<br>(150) |
| 20. | Injena | – | 412 | 65.93<br>(1258) | 0.31<br>(6) | 33.75<br>(644) | 100.00<br>(1908) |
| 21. | Chandaka | – | 384 | 15.22<br>(305) | 13.97<br>(280) | 70.81<br>(1419) | 100.00<br>(2004) |
| | **Average** | | **269** | **393.23** | **92.67** | **1003.84** | **1489.61** |

*Note:* *(i)* Nathapur (sl. No. 16) is included in Lingipur

*(ii)* Excluding Tankapani, Kantunia and Rahadamunda

*Sources:* Villages census abstract (unpublished), census office, Bhubaneswar.

# Appendix—3

## LITERACY AMONG VILLAGE-WISE POPULATION

| *Sl. No.* | *Village* | *Total Population* | *Literate* | *% age to total population* | *Illiterate* | *% age to total population* |
|---|---|---|---|---|---|---|
| *(1)* | *(2)* | *(3)* | *(4)* | *(5)* | *(6)* | *(7)* |
| 1. | Balianta | 2850 | 1760 | 61.75 | 1090 | 38.25 |
| 2. | Satyabhamapur | 580 | 273 | 47.07 | 307 | 52.93 |
| 3. | Bhubanpur | 2713 | 616 | 22.71 | 2097 | 77.29 |
| 4. | Gotalagram | 889 | 483 | 54.33 | 406 | 45.67 |
| 5. | G. Srirampur | 597 | 350 | 58.63 | 247 | 41.37 |
| 6. | Andilo | 1843 | 898 | 48.72 | 945 | 51.28 |
| 7. | Tankapani | – | – | – | – | – |
| 8. | Bhainchua | 3509 | 1615 | 46.02 | 1894 | 53.98 |
| 9. | Kanturia | – | – | – | – | – |
| 10. | Rahadamunda | – | – | – | – | – |
| 11. | Jasuapur | 760 | 386 | 50.79 | 374 | 49.21 |
| 12. | Indrapal | 818 | 358 | 43.77 | 460 | 56.23 |
| 13. | Bikipur | 289 | 163 | 56.40 | 126 | 43.60 |
| 14. | Itipur | 318 | 176 | 55.35 | 142 | 44.65 |
| 15. | Jaipur | 260 | 156 | 60.00 | 104 | 40.00 |
| 16. | Nathapur | 1909 | 1337 | 70.04 | 572 | 29.96 |
| 17. | Raghunathpur | 2564 | 1004 | 39.16 | 1560 | 60.84 |
| 18. | Daruthenga | 2852 | 1424 | 49.93 | 1428 | 50.07 |
| 19. | Damodarpur | 150 | 115 | 76.67 | 35 | 23.33 |
| 20. | Injena | 1908 | 697 | 36.53 | 1211 | 63.47 |
| 21. | Chandaka | 2004 | 969 | 48.35 | 1035 | 51.65 |

*Note and Source:* As per Table 3.1.

# Appendix—4

## DISTRIBUTION OF PENSIONERS ACCORDING TO LAST POST HELD

| *Govt.* | *Department/ institution* | *Frequency* | *Post held* |
|---|---|---|---|
| *(1)* | *(2)* | *(3)* | *(4)* |
| State | Agriculture | 2 | VLW-1, Library Attendant-1 |
| | Animal Husbandry | 1 | Veterinary Technician |
| | Co-operation | 1 | Inspector of Co-operatives |
| | Culture | 1 | Head mali |
| | Directorate of Treasuries | 1 | Sr. Asst. |
| | Education | 5 | Head Master-4 Library Attendant |
| | Home | 7 | Auditor-1, Habildar-2, Sub-Inspector-1, Constable |
| | Irrigation | 7 | Pump Driver-1, Peon-1, Khalasi-4, Water man-1 |
| | Planning and Co-ordination | 1 | Moharir |
| | Revenue | 4 | Survey Inspector-1, Head Asst.-1, Peon-1 |
| | Public Health (Medical) | 3 | Section Officer-1, Leprosy Asst.-1, Peon-1 |
| | Public Health (Water) | 1 | Sr. Asst. |
| | Rural Works | 1 | Office Superintendent |

*(Contd...)*

| *(1)* | *(2)* | *(3)* | *(4)* |
|---|---|---|---|
| | PWD and R and B | 2 | Sr. Progress Recorder-1<br>Sr. Clerk-1 |
| | Water Resource | 1 | Section Officer |
| | Statistics | 1 | Statistical Investigator |
| Union | Income Tax | 1 | Note Server |
| | Post and Telegraph | 1 | Post Master |
| | Railways | 12 | Constable-1, Train Driver-1, Keyman-2, Khalasi-1, Mate-1,<br>Watchman-1, Gangman-3, Choukidar-1 |
| | RBI | 2 | Mechanic-1, Electrician-1 |

# Appendix—5

**DISTRIBUTION OF AGED DOING PRIVATE JOB, BUSINESS ACCORDING TO TYPE OF JOBS**

| *Occupation* | *Frequency* | *Type of Job* |
|---|---|---|
| *(1)* | *(2)* | *(3)* |
| Private job | 3 | Yard Gunner-1, Sewing Instructor-2 |
| Business | 3 | Hotel Business-1 Vegetable Business-2, Potato-selling |
| Agriculture | 3 | Small/Marginal Farmer |
| Wage-earning | 3 | Agricultural |

# Appendix—6

## DISTRIBUTION OF FAMILY-PENSION HOLDERS ACCORDING TO LAST POST HELD BY THEIR HUSBANDS

| *Govt.* | *Department/ Institution* | *Frequency* | *Post held* |
|---|---|---|---|
| *(1)* | *(2)* | *(3)* | *(4)* |
| State | Civil supply | 1 | Attendant-1 |
| | Agriculture | 1 | Choukidar-1 |
| | Home | 3 | Constable-2, Habildar-1 |
| | Irrigation | 6 | Peon-5, Khalasi-1 |
| | Finance | 2 | Peon-2 |
| | Revenue | 2 | Amin-1, Revenue Inspector-1 |
| | Public Health | 1 | Choukidar |
| Union | Geological Survey of India | 1 | Watchman |
| | Railways | 4 | Khalsai-1, Gangman-3 |

# Appendix—7

## BALANCED DIET FOR AN AGED MAN AND WOMAN PER DAY

| *Foodstuffs* | *Quantity (raw) Gms* | |
|---|---|---|
| | *Male* | *Female* |
| *(1)* | *(2)* | *(3)* |
| Cereal | 350 | 225 |
| Pulses | 50 | 40 |
| Vegetables | 200 | 150 |
| Green leafy vegetables | 50 | 50 |
| Roots and tubers | 100 | 100 |
| Fruits | 200 | 200 |
| Milk and milk products | 300 | 300 |
| Sugar | 20 | 20 |
| Fats and oil | 25 | 20 |
| Approximate nutriets supplied calories | 2200 | 1700 |
| Protein | 65 g | 50 g |
| Fat | 50 g | 40 g |
| Calcium | 1 g | 0.9 g |
| Iron | 38 mg | 30 mg |
| Vitamin A (Retionol) | 1030 mg | 930 mg |
| Thiamin | 1.96 mg | 1.45 mg |
| Riboflabin | 1.78 mg | 1.51 mg |

*Source:* Pasricha and Thimmayamaa, 1997, p. 7.

# Appendix—8

## NO. OF PENSIONERS AT DISTRICT TREASURY, KHURDHA (AS ON 30.4.98)

| *Sl. No.* | *Category of pensioners* | *Treasury* | *Public sector banks* | *Total* |
|---|---|---|---|---|
| *(1)* | *(2)* | *(3)* | *(4)* | *(5)* |
| 1. | Service | 3528 | 2685 | 6213 |
| 2. | Family-pension-holders | 1139 | 885 | 2024 |
| 3. | T B S | 25 | 8 | 33 |
| 4. | T P S | 71 | 31 | 102 |
| 5. | M L A | 58 | 92 | 150 |
| 6. | State freedom fighter | 39 | 72 | 111 |
| 7. | Swatantra Sanmman (SS) | 25 | 42 | 67 |
| 8. | Military | 178 | 227 | 405 |
| 9. | Railways | 25 | 38 | 63 |
| 10. | Central Govt. Pensioners | 15 | 8 | 23 |
| 11. | Central family-pension-holders | 8 | 5 | 13 |
| 12. | West Bengal pensioners | 27 | 22 | 49 |
| 13. | Andhra Pradesh pensioners | 2 | 1 | 3 |
| 14. | Bihar pensioners | 1 | 1 | 2 |
| 15. | Nagaland pensioners | 1 | 1 | 2 |
| 16. | Assam pensioners | 2 | 1 | 3 |
| 17. | Manipur pensioners | 2 | 1 | 3 |
| | **Total** | **5146 (62.26)** | **3120 (37.74)** | **8266 (100.00)** |

*Source:* District Treasury, Khurdha.

# Appendix—9

## DATES FOR DRAWAL OF PENSION AMONG DIFFERENT CATEGORY OF PENSIONERS

| *Date (working days)* | *Category of pensioners* |
|---|---|
| *(1)* | *(2)* |
| 1st-3rd | Retired pensioners |
| 4th-5th | Family-pension-holders |
| 6th-7th | Freedom fighters (State + Central) |
| 8th-9th | Railway and other state (Other than Orissa) |
| 10th | Teacher's Pensioners |
| 11th onwards | Arrear |

*Source:* District Treasury, Khurdha.

# Appendix—10

## DISTRICT-WISE TARGET OF PENSIONERS UNDER NATIONAL OLD-AGE PENSION SCHEME IN ORISSA (1998-99)

| *Sl. No.* | *Name of districts* | *Target* | *% age to total* |
|---|---|---|---|
| *(1)* | *(2)* | *(3)* | *(4)* |
| 1. | Angul | 8603 | 2.58 |
| 2. | Balasore | 15187 | 4.56 |
| 3. | Bargarh | 10806 | 3.24 |
| 4. | Bhadrak | 9899 | 2.97 |
| 5. | Boudh | 2843 | 0.85 |
| 6. | Bolangir | 20750 | 6.22 |
| 7. | Cuttack | 17659 | 5.30 |
| 8. | Debgarh | 2097 | 0.63 |
| 9. | Dhenkanal | 8485 | 2.54 |
| 10. | Gajapati | 4070 | 1.22 |
| 11. | Ganjam | 24205 | 7.26 |
| 12. | Jagatsingpur | 9079 | 2.72 |
| 13. | Jajpur | 12408 | 3.72 |
| 14. | Jharsuguda | 3998 | 1.20 |
| 15. | Kalahandi | 19066 | 5.72 |
| 16. | Kendrapara | 10290 | 3.09 |

*(Contd...)*

| (1) | (2) | (3) | (4) |
|---|---|---|---|
| 17. | Keonjhar | 10968 | 3.29 |
| 18. | Khurdha | 13445 | 4.03 |
| 19. | Koraput | 17333 | 5.20 |
| 20. | Malkangiri | 7150 | 2.14 |
| 21. | Mayurbhanj | 16872 | 5.06 |
| 22. | Nabarangpur | 14280 | 4.28 |
| 23. | Nayagarh | 7006 | 2.10 |
| 24. | Nuapada | 7914 | 2.37 |
| 25. | Phulbani | 4888 | 1.47 |
| 26. | Puri | 11685 | 3.50 |
| 27. | Rayagada | 12042 | 3.61 |
| 28. | Sambalpur | 7242 | 2.17 |
| 29. | Sonpur | 8044 | 2.41 |
| 30. | Sundargarh | 14086 | 4.22 |
| | **Total** | **333400** | **100.00** |

*Source:* Office Files of Social Defence Section, Women and Child Welfare Department, Govt. of Orissa.

# Appendix—11

**LIST OF MOBILE MEDICARE CENTRES UNDER GOVT. OF INDIA SCHEME**

| *Sl. No.* | *Name of the organisation* | *Location of the project* | *Date of commencement* |
|---|---|---|---|
| *(1)* | *(2)* | *(3)* | *(4)* |
| 1. | Organisation of Social Change and Rural Development (OSCARD), A/85, Sahid Nagar, Bhubaneswar | A/85, Sahid Nagar, Bhubaneswar | 1.4.94 |
| 2. | Orissa Association for Deaf, 105/A, Palashpalli, Aerodrome Area, Bhubaneswar | 105/A, Palaspalli, Aerodrome Area, Bhubaneswar | 1.9.98 |
| 3. | Union of Learning Training and Reformative Activities, (ULTRA), At/PO- Sagargaon, Via- Rajsunakhala, Dist- Khurdha | At/PO- Sagargaon, Via- Rajsunakhala, Dist- Khurdha | 1.12.98 |

*Source:* Handicapped Section, Dept. of Women and Child Welfare, Govt. of India.

# Appendix—12

## LIST OF DAY-CARE CENTRES FUNCTIONING IN THE STATE ORISSA FOR THE WELFARE OF THE AGED UNDER GOVT. OF INDIA SCHEME

| *Sl. No.* | *Name of the organisation running the project* | *Location of the day care centre for the aged* | *Date of commencement* | *No. of beneficiaries* |
|---|---|---|---|---|
| *(1)* | *(2)* | *(3)* | *(4)* | *(5)* |
| 1. | Grama Seva Mandal, At/P.O.- Hakimpada, | Senilichhain, Dist- Angul | 31.3.87 | 150 |
| 2. | -do- | Mahidharpur, Dist- Angul | 1.4.87 | 150 |
| 3. | -do- | Bagada, Dist- Dhenkanal | 1.4.87 | 150 |
| 4. | -do- | Kantamila Dist- Dhenkanal | 1.4.87 | 150 |
| 5. | -do- | Rakla, Dist- Dhenkanal | 1.4.87 | 150 |
| 6. | -do- | Angul N.A.C | 31.3.94 | 150 |
| 7. | Manab Seva Sadan, At/PO- Saranga, Dist- Dhenkanal | Saranga, P.O- Saranga, Dist- Dhenkanal | 1.2.95 | 150 |

*(Contd...)*

| (1) | (2) | (3) | (4) | (5) |
|---|---|---|---|---|
| 8. | Ashanayakam Seva Sangha, At- Benjarapur P.O- Mandari, Via- Bari, Dist- Jajpur | Kampagarh, P.O- Kampagarh, Via- Bari, Dist- Jajpur | 10.10.79 | 150 |
| 9. | Ashanayakam Seva Sangha, At- Benjarapur, P.O- Mandari, Via- Bari Dist- Jajpur | Routsahi P.O- Routsahi, Via- Bari, Dist- Jajpur | 10.10.79 | 150 |
| 10. | -do- | Aliabad, P.O- Ratnagiri Via- Bari, Dist- Jajpur | 10.10.79 | 150 |
| 11. | -do- | Hatasahi, P.O- Mandari, Via- Bari, Dis- Jajpur | 10.10.79 | 150 |
| 12. | -do- | Srirampur, P.O- Serpur, Via- Bari, Dist- Jajpur | 10.10.79 | 150 |
| 13. | Bhairabi Club, At- Karumpada, P.O- Hadapada, Via- Narangarh, Dist- Khurda | Narangarh, Dist- Khurda | 1.11.93 | 150 |
| 14. | Singhanath Club, At- Teleania, P.O- Bongarsingha, Dist- Cuttack | Bangarsingha, Y.P. P.O- Bangarsingha, Dist- Cuttack | 16.3.91 | |
| 15. | Janakalyana Samiti, Plot No. 1550, Bhimatangi, Bhubaneswar, Dist- Khurda | Plot No.- 1550 Bhimatangi, Bhubaneswar, Dist- Khurda | 1.4.91 | 150 |
| 16. | -do- | Ienthakata, Bhudan Nagar, Puri-Municipality, Dist- Puri | 1.4.91 | 150 |

*(Contd...)*

| (1) | (2) | (3) | (4) | (5) |
|---|---|---|---|---|
| 17. | -do- | Pattaangi, Dist- Koraput | 1.4.91 | 150 |
| 18. | -do- | Rayagada | 1.4.91 | 150 |
| 19. | Kalinga Shelter, B/22-Indradhanu Market, Complex, Nayapalli, Bhubaneswar, Dist- Khurda. | Ghatikia, Bhubaneswar Dist- Khurda | 15.8.90 | 150 |
| 20. | Social Welfare Organisation and Research Group, Plot No. 106- Jayadev Vihar, Bidyut Marg BBSR- 751013 | DL- 39, V.S.S. Nagar, Bhubaneswar, Dist- Khurda | 1.9.98 | 150 |
| 21. | Organisation for Social Change for Rural Development, A/85- Sahid Nagar, Bhubaneswar | Chhatabar, Jatni, Dist- Khurda | 1.4.92 | 150 |
| 22. | Organisation for Social Change and Rural Development, A/85- Sahid Nagar, Bhubaneswar, Dist- Khurda | Saliasahi Bhubaneswar, Dist- Khurda Plot No. 643, Nayapalli | 1.4.92 | 150 |
| 23. | Viswa Jeevan Seva Sangh, At/P.O- Saradhapur, Dist- Khurda | Saradhapur, Dist- Khurda | 1.2.94 | 150 |
| 24. | Jayjaganath Club, At/P.O- Badaberna, Dist- Khurda | At/PO- Badaberava, Dist- Khurda | 1.3.92 | 150 |
| 25. | Bapujee Jubak Sangh, At/P.O- Bolagarh, Dist- Khurda | Bolagarh, Dist- Khurda | 1.12.94 | 150 |
| 26. | Students Welfare Institute A-4/7-IE-IRC Village Bhubaneswar, Dist- Khurda | Jhinti Sasan, Khurda | 1.9.93 | 150 |

*(Contd...)*

| (1) | (2) | (3) | (4) | (5) |
|---|---|---|---|---|
| 27. | Bahubachan, i-Ganganagar Bhubaneswar, Dist- Khurda | Ganganagar, Bhubaneswar, Dist- Khurda | April, 95 | 150 |
| 28. | Association for Under Developed Beneficiaries of India, Gambharidihi, Dist- Nayagarh | Nayagarh | 1.6.93 | 150 |
| 29. | Nilachal Seva Pratisthan Dayavihar, Konas, Dist- Puri | Village- Tikina, Konark, Dist- Puri | 1.12.93 | 150 |
| 30. | Sri Sri Balikapileswar Yuba Sangha and Pathagarh, At- Dampur P.O- Berboi, Dist- Puri | Berboi Delang, Dist- Puri | 1.6.93 | 150 |
| 31. | Subhadra Mahatab Seva Sadan, At/P.O- G. Udayagiri, Dist- Phulbani | Hill Patna Berhampur, Dist- Ganjam | March 91 | 150 |
| 32. | Bidyut Club, At- Haladiapada, Lokpal, P.O- Haldiapada, Dist- Puri | Ghoradia, P.O- Gharadia, (Delanga) Dist- Puri | 1.4.93 | 150 |
| 33. | -do- | Kalyanpur P.O- Kalyanpur, Delanga, Dist- Puri | 1.4.93 | 150 |
| 34. | -do- | Tirimal, P.O- Tirimal, Jatni, Dist- Khurda | 1.4.93 | 150 |
| 35. | Bidyut Club At- Haladiapada, Lokpal, P.O- Haladiapada, Dist- Puri | Taraboi, P.O- Taraboi, (Jatni) Dist- Khurda | 1.4.93 | 150 |

(Contd...)

| (1) | (2) | (3) | (4) | (5) |
|---|---|---|---|---|
| 36. | -do- | Gangapada, P.O- Gangapada, Jatni Dist- Khurda | 1.4.93 | 150 |
| 37. | Maharsi Dayananda Service Mission At/P.O- Joranda, Dist- Dhenkanal | At- Kaluria, Goindia Block of DKL Dist. | 1.12.98 | 150 |
| 38. | -do- | Mahapada, in Goindia Block of DKL Dist. | -do- | 150 |
| 39. | -do- | At- Joranda in Goindia Block of DKL Dist. | -do- | 150 |
| 40. | -do- | At- Chudakhaia, in Goindia Block of DKL Dist. | -do- | 150 |
| 41. | Council for all Round Development Society, 5212 Badagada, BBSR-18 | Old Town, B B S R | 1.11.98 | 150 |
| 42. | -do- | Raghunathnagar, Slum Duinduma Housing Board, BBSR | 1.11.98 | 150 |
| 43. | Union of Learning Training and Reformative Activities (ULTRA) At/P.O- Sagargoan, Via- Rajsunakhala, Dist- Khurda | At- Jaripada, P.O- Sagargoan, Dist- Khurda | 1.12.98 | 150 |
| 44. | Tribal Development Association of Indian Institutes, (TDAII) L-1/492, Phase-III, Dumduma Housing Board Colony, BBSR | Nuapada, | 1.12.98 | 150 |

*(Contd...)*

| (1) | (2) | (3) | (4) | (5) |
|---|---|---|---|---|
| 45. | -do- | Bhawanipatna. | 1.12.98 | 150 |
| 46. | Orissa Multipurpose Development Centre 4/14 MIG-II, BDA Colony, Chandrasekharpur, BBSR | At/P.O- Nandipur, Via- Yaradapur, Dist-Kendrapara | 1.10.98 | 150 |
| 47. | Orissa Association for Deaf, 105/A, Palashpalli, Areodrome Area, BBSR | 105/A, Palashpalli, BBSR | 1-9.98 | |
| 48. | Luthuan Mahila Samiti, At/P.O- Patalipanka, Via- Kunjanga Dist- Kendrapara | At/P.o- Pataliponka, Via- Kujangh, Dist- Kenderapara | 1.9.98 | 150 |
| 49. | Community Legal Action and Research Centre (CLARC) At- Gobardhanpur, P.O- Karamal, Dist- Dhenkanal | At- Jaripada, Chendipada Block of Angul Dist. | 1.10.98 | 150 |
| 50. | -do- | At- Tukuda, Chendipada Block of Angul Dist. | 1.10.98 | 150 |
| 51. | -do- | At- Durgapur, Chendipada Block of Angul Dist. | 1.10.98 | 150 |
| 52. | -do- | At-Jaranga, Chendipara Block of Angul Dist. | 1.10.98 | 150 |

# Appendix—13

## LIST OF OLD-AGE HOMES UNDER GOVT. OF INDIA SCHEME

| *Sl. No.* | *Name and detailed Address of the organisation* | *Location of the project* | *Date of commencement of the project* | *No. of Beneficiaries* |
|---|---|---|---|---|
| *(1)* | *(2)* | *(3)* | *(4)* | *(5)* |
| 1. | Janakalyan Samiti, Plot No. 1550, Bhimatangi, BBSR | At- Padwa, Nandapur, Block Dist- Koraput | 1.7.91 | 25 |
| 2. | Association for Social Reconstructive Activities (ASRA), Satyabrata Press Premises, Pithapur, Cuttack | At/P.O- Ichhapur, Balikuda, Jagatsingpur | 1.12.93 | 25 |
| 3. | Grama Seva Mandal At/P.O- Hakimpara, Dist- Angul | Similichhuin, Banarpal Block, Dist- Angul | 1.10.93 | 25 |
| 4. | Gram Mangal Pathagar, At/P.O- Salepali, Dist- Bolangir | At/P.O- Salepali, Bolangir. | 1.7.93 | 25 |
| 5. | Lok Nayak Club, At/P.O- Banki, Dist- Cuttack | At/P.O- Patapur, Via- Banki, Dist- Cuttack | 1.1.91 | 25 |

*(Contd...)*

| (1) | (2) | (3) | (4) | (5) |
|---|---|---|---|---|
| 6. | Subhadra Mahatab Seva Sadan, At/P.O- G. Udayagiri | Gopalpur Sea Beach | 1.9.90 | 25 |
| 7. | Institute for Wemen Welfare Court Peta, (Berhampur) Dist- Ganjam | Gajapati Nagar, 10th Line, Berhampur, Dist- Ganjam | 1.9.90 | 35 |
| 8. | Janaseva Parishad, Abhaya Bhawan, Post/Dist- Kendrapara | At/P.O- Kendrapara, Dist- Kendrapara | 1.4.95 | 25 |
| 9. | Bhairabi Club, At- Kurumpara, P.o- Hadapada, Via- Narangarh, Dist- Khurda | At/P.O- Narangarh, Dist- Khurda | 1.9.91 | 25 |
| 10. | Kalinga Shelter, B/22- Indradhanu Market Complex Nayapalli, BBSR, Dist- Khurda | Bhubaneswar, Dist- Khurda | 1.3.94 | 25 |
| 11. | Janjyoti Club, At- Kumandal P.O- Nairi, Dist- Khurda | Kumandal P.O- Nairi, Dist- Khurda | 1.12.94 | 25 |
| 12. | Nilachal Seva Pratisthan, Dayavihar, Dist- Puri | Dayavihar, Kanas, Dist- Puri | 1.4.91 | 25 |
| 13. | -do- | Sea Beach, Puri. | 1.12.93 | 25 |
| 14. | Organisation of Social Change and Rural Development (OSCARD) A/85- Sahid Nagar, Bhubaneswar, Dist- Khurda | Jeenchi, Konark N.A.C., Dist- Puri. | 1.4.94 | 25 |

(Contd...)

| (1) | (2) | (3) | (4) | (5) |
|---|---|---|---|---|
| 15. | Banabasi Seva Samiti, At/P.O- Baliguda, Dist- Phulbani | Baliguda, Phulbani. | 1.8.90 | 25 |
| 16. | Association for Social Work and Social Research in Orissa, 16, Satyanagar, Bhubaneswar, Dist- Khurda | Kothagarh Dist- Phulbani | 1.4.92 | 25 |
| 17. | Ratnachira, At/P.O- Satasankha, Dist- Puri | Satasankha P.O- Jasuapur, Pipili Block, Dist- Puri. | 8.2.95 | 25 |
| 18. | Sri Sri Balika-pileswar Yuba Sangh and Pathagar, P.O- Berboi Dist- Puri | At- Danpur, P.O- Berboi Delang Block, Dist- Puri | 1.2.95 | 25 |
| 19. | Sri Ramakrishna Ashram, M. Rampur Bhawanipatna, Dist- Kalahandi | M. Rampur, Bhawanipatna | 1.3.96 (Discon-tinued) This started during Sept. 1996 | 35 |
| 20. | Maharsi Dayananda Service Mission, At/P.O.- Joranda Dist- Dhenkanal | At- Pingua, in Govinda Block of Dhenkanal | 1.12.98 | 25 |
| 21. | Union for Learning Training and Reformative Activities (ULTRA) At/P.O- Sagargoan, Via- Rajsunakhala, Dist- Khurda | At/P.O- Sagargon, Dist- Khurda | 1.12.98 | 25 |
| 22. | Community Legal Action and Research Centre (CLARC) At- Gobardhanpur, P.O- Karamal, Dist- Dhenkanal. | At- Jarapada, in Chhendipada Block of Angul Dist. | 1.10.98 | 25 |

(Contd...)

| (1) | (2) | (3) | (4) | (5) |
|---|---|---|---|---|
| 23. | Tribal Development Association of Indian Institute (TDAII) L-I/492, Phase-III, Dumduma Housing Board Colony, BBSR | Nuapada | 1.12.98 | 25 |
| 24. | Surkhya, Police Line, Puri | Srikhetra Colony, Puri | 1.8.98 | 25 |
| 25. | Orissa Association for Deaf, 105/A, Palashpalli, Aerodrome Area, BBSR | 105/A, Palashapalli, BBSR. | 1.9.98 | 25 |
| 26. | Cutheran Mahila Samiti, At/P.O.- Pataliarka, Via- Kujanga Dist.- Kendrapara | At/P.O- Pataliparka, Via- Kujanga, Dist- Kendrapara | 1.9.98 | 25 |

# Appendix—14

## LIST OF OLD-AGE HOMES RUN OUT OF GOVT. OF ORISSA FUND

| *Sl. No.* | *Name of the organisation* | *Location of project* | *No. of beneficiaries* |
|---|---|---|---|
| *(1)* | *(2)* | *(3)* | *(4)* |
| 1. | Association for Social Reconstructive Activities, Pithapur, Cuttack | Raghunathpur, Jagatsinghpur, district | 25 |
| 2. | Patitapaban Seva Sangha, Nimapara, Dist. Puri | Nimapara | 25 |

# Appendix—15

## DISTRICT-WISE TARGET OF PENSIONERS UNDER OLD-AGE PENSION SCHEME OF GOVT. OF ORISSA (1998-99)

| *Sl. No.* | *Name of the district* | *Target* | *% age to total* |
|---|---|---|---|
| *(1)* | *(2)* | *(3)* | *(4)* |
| 1. | Angul | 15664 | 2.67 |
| 2. | Balasore | 21730 | 4.12 |
| 3. | Bhadrak | 18502 | 3.50 |
| 4. | Balangir | 22022 | 4.17 |
| 5. | Bargarh | 17950 | 3.40 |
| 6. | Boudh | 5036 | 0.95 |
| 7. | Cuttack | 39320 | 7.45 |
| 8. | Dhenkanal | 17006 | 3.22 |
| 9. | Deogarh | 4511 | 0.85 |
| 10. | Ganjam | 38893 | 7.37 |
| 11. | Gajapati | 9284 | 1.76 |
| 12. | Jagaraingpur | 15954 | 3.02 |
| 13. | Jajpur | 15603 | 2.96 |
| 14. | Jharsuguda | 5635 | 1.07 |
| 15. | Kalahandi | 39514 | 7.48 |
| 16. | Keonjhar | 19256 | 3.65 |
| 17. | Koraput | 18810 | 3.56 |

*(Contd...)*

| (1) | (2) | (3) | (4) |
|---|---|---|---|
| 18. | Kendrapara | 27961 | 5.30 |
| 19. | Khurda | 18572 | 3.52 |
| 20. | Malkangiri | 9732 | 1.84 |
| 21. | Mayurbhanj | 28304 | 5.36 |
| 22. | Nabarangpur | 16769 | 3.18 |
| 23. | Nayagarh | 13264 | 2.51 |
| 24. | Nuapara | 13419 | 2.54 |
| 25. | Puri | 12964 | 2.46 |
| 26. | Phulbani | 12494 | 2.37 |
| 27. | Rayagada | 14713 | 2.79 |
| 28. | Sonpur | 6697 | 1.27 |
| 29. | Sambalpur | 12834 | 2.43 |
| 30. | Sundargarh | 15579 | 2.95 |
| | **Total** | **528000** | **100.00** |

*Source:* Office Files of Social Defence Section, Women and Child Welfare Department, Govt. of Orissa.

# Appendix—16

## CASE STUDIES

### Case Study: 1

Digambar Ojha is a man of about 80-years-old and his wife Malati is approximately of 68 years. He resides in the village Gotalagram under Balianta block of Khurdha district. He is *Kamara* (black smith) by caste.

He is a very poor man. He was working as a wage-earner but now unable to work as such and earn. He depends on his wife for his survival. His wife is working in some way or other depending upon the availability of the work. However, he and his wife are getting Rs. 100/- each per month as old-age pension from the local block office. But this paltry sum is far too less to meet their basic requirements.

Digambar did not have any child of his own. So he had adopted Gadadhar (3rd son of his mother's sister) with a hope that he would look after him and his wife during their old age.

Gadhadhar was only 3-months-old when he came to the house of Digambar as an adopted son. Digambar and Malati devoted their whole life for the well-being of Gadadhar and led a happy life. Gadadhar was brought up with all possible care by Digambar and his wife. His foster parents arranged for his marriage. Digambar had only half an acre of agricultural land, which he had to sell in order to perform the marriage ceremony of Gadadhar with pomp and grandeur, so that none would feel that Digambar spent less money in the marriage ceremony of Gadadhar as he was not his own son. But as ill luck would have it, after the marriage of Gadadhar, the situation of Digambar and his wife started becoming miserable and the situation worsened day by day. Janha, wife of Gadadhar started playing a nefarious in order to get separated from her parents-in-law and lead life independently with her husband. In course of time, Gadadhar supported his wife and both of them created more and more conflicting situations with the old couple and it became intolerable for them. The mental agony of Digambar and his wife increased and they started loosening the tranquility of their mind. One day, in a tense situation, Gadadhar told his foster parents that "You useless persons have become an encumbrance for us and I do not have ability to feed you. Now, I have my own family. Earn for yourself and take your own responsibility". Finally, they got separated from each other in 1988. Since then, Digambar and his wife are leading a harsh life alone in a small room. They earn for themselves and there is nobody to look after them. Whenever they fall ill, they spend their own money for treatment otherwise remain as such.

While sharing some of their personal feelings with the investigator, Digambar's wife said "Listen my son, (their son and his wife) are so cruel and heartless that they do not permit our grandchildren to mix with us. They want that we must die as soon as it happens since we have become old and do not have any regular source of income. Gadadhar changed drastically after we lost our property. If we had some property now, we are sure, he would have looked after us. Now his intention is quite clear. God is there to his low justice". Digambar said "blood attracts blood". By this he meant children of own blood would be helpful to their parents in old age. Others may or may not care for.

More or less a similar type of case comes from the village Tankapani of the same block. But in this case, the adopted son remaining very loyal and obliged to his foster parents. The most disturbing element that procedure desperate situations, is solely the wife of the adopted son. The case is described below.

**Case Study: 2**

Duryodhan Panda is about 80-years-old. He is a widower and *Brahman* (priest) by caste. He belongs to the village Tankapani of Balianta block.

Duryodhan was running a hotel in Bhubaneswar city in 1960s. He had no issue. So he adopted a poor *Brahman* boy as his son in 1967. This boy was working as an assistant in his hotel.

For some reasons, Duryodhan lost his hotel business in 1980. He has now retired from his active life, and in a way is bedridden. He suffers from asthma. He stays on the outer verandah of his front house where sack screens have been provided to protect him from the outside.

Duryodhan's son is the only earning member in his family. He sells lemon in the daily market of Bhubaneswar. Duryodhan says that, "my son is very good. He is very kind-hearted and his heart is as clear as a crystal. After all he is a piece of gold and there is no son like him. He works very hard. Every morning, he goes to Bhubaneswar in connection with his business and comes back in the evening. He respects me and obeys me. His reverence towards me is unique and be an example for others. But what happens? His own wife is not learning anything from her obedient husband. She has come from an uncultured family. Of course this is my fault. It was I who forced my son to marry this lady. Now I repent and I raise that this little mistake has shattered my pious wish to built a happy home". Further he also expressed his agony and unhappiness in the following manner.

"My daughter-in-law is a very hard spoken woman. She does not respect me. Sometimes she abuses me in filthy language, pouts and openly says that I must die soon so that she would be relieved of drudgery. She is very intelligent and a cunning lady. She is so tactful that she never misbehaves with me in front of my son rather acts as if she is caring for me with utmost sincerity. Once my son goes out of home, she becomes all in all and I become a subordinate in the family. My presence becomes futile. My authority is snatched away and in that case I am not even allowed to employ a coconut plucker to pluck a green coconut from my own tree which I have planted. What is more surprising is that my son brings some snacks for me; at least three times a week. But unfortunately my share becomes least. Some-days my son also gives me Rs. 5/- to purchase snacks. I get it through my grandchildren and we all share it. But most often my daughter-in-law snatches away the money and either purchases some commodities or keeps with her. However, all these happen without the knowledge of my son otherwise there would be open conflict between them. In order to avoid unpleasant situations, I suppress all these and try to forget what my daughter-in-law does. But her repeated uncivil and odious behaviour has increased my mental agony and I have become unflappable. I get happiness only when my son comes back from work... He likes me and I also like him. My grandchildren are very loving and polite. They do not bear upon my distress condition and sometimes they oppose their mother for her disregard to me.

Fortunately, I could have a short conversation with Duryodhan when his daughter-in-law was busy in washing clothes at the nearby pond.

It is not only Duryodhan, but many more like him who are now in this state of misery which must be wiped out through consciousness and arousal of moral values.

**Case Study: 3**

Nidhi Sahoo is a man of about 65-yerars-old. He resides in Gotalagram under Balianta block of Khurdha district.

Nidhi has one daughter but does not have son of his own. According to him, in a patrilineal society like ours, one must have a son who is required to perform the death rites and perform death anniversary rituals, otherwise a person does not get salvation after his/her death. This factor led him to adopt his nephew (sister's son) as his son. He had also hoped that his son would be a blindman's stick during his old age. But unfortunately his hope has remained as a hope since his adopted son was separated from his after few years of his marriage. Now Nidhi does not have any social relationship with him.

Nidhi's daughter got married to Maguni Swain. She has five children. Of these, three are daughters and the rest two are sons. Two of her daughters are married.

In 1989, Maguni became mad and now he is a wanderer and runs from street to street. After that Gauri is staying permanently with all her unmarried children at Gotalgram at his father's house. Nidhi's adopted son and his daughter-in-law opposed their staying there but Nidhi liked to keep his daughter and grandchildren (daughter's children) with him. This resulted in separation of Nidhi's adopted son from him. Now his son is staying at the village site. He has constructed a new house on an agricultural land which Nidhi had transferred to his (Maguni's) name after adoption. Nidhi's son enjoys the whole piece of land and does not give any share of the crop produced in it to Nidhi. So, even if Nidhi is now old and is a physically weak person, he has to labour hard for managing his family.

Nidhi has taken to a strenuous job like paddy processing and selling of rice in the local markets. His wife and daughter help him in his business.

His wife speaks that they have made a great blunder by adopting their nephew. They feel that it would have been beneficial for them if they had adopted one of their grandchildren (daughter's children) who are now staying with them.

Nidhi's wife shared many of her sorrowful feelings with the investigator which she had experienced while staying with her adopted son. Even if they are now leading life separately from their son, they are not free from the ill treatment of their son and daughter-in-law. She claims that they are harassed in many ways; both directly and indirectly. Their son and daughter-in-law do not have talking relationship with them. Their grandchildren (adopted son's children) also do not talk to them. Whenever they visit to them and are detected by their parents, they are either scolded or beaten up. Moreover, in order to irritate them, their son wilfully prepares sweets and cakes on various festive occasions and distributes among the neighbours but never cares for his old foster parents. All these contemptuous behaviour became very unbearable from them and they spend their time in a very disturbed state of mind which is not generally perspicacious to the public.

**Case Study: 4**

Sanatan Sahoo of Gotalagram is about 70-years-old. His wife Sauri is aged 63 years. She is mad. Sanatan is *Teli* (oil crusher) by caste.

Sanatan has one son and three daughters. All his children are married except one daughter. Sanatan has a strained relationship with his son. One day his son told him "*Nije Viao Nije Chala. Mun Tumaku Posi Paribini*". By this, he meant "work for yourself. I am unable to feed you". Since that day they have been separated from each other and lead life independently.

Sanatan has 40 decimal of agricultural land. He cultivates this patch of land but the income from this source is not sufficient. As a result, he works as a wage-earner to supplement his income. He also gets Rs. 100/- per month as old-age pension which he saves for the purpose of the marriage of his daughter. He said that his son had told him that he would not help him in any manner. So, now, he works hard day and night and is mentally upset and perturbed about the marriage of his daughter.

Sanatan further said that his son does not pay money to meet the social necessities, like birth rites, death rituals or marriage ceremonies of his relatives. However, his son manages his own affines. Sanatan is distressed with this sort of life. So, now he intends to die. The only thing left for his son is that he should put few drops of water in the mouth of his father at dying moments. By doing this, Sanatan specifies that his soul would get salvation.

**Cast Study: 5**

Prafulla Chandra Das is a man of 74-years-old. He is *Karan* (scribe) by caste. He resides in the village Satyabhamapur. This is situated in Balianta block of Khurdha district.

He is a matriculate. He was serving as a Sub-Inspector of police under government of Orissa and has retired from service in 1982. Now he gets Rs. 2462/- per month as his pension.

He has six daughters and five sons. They are all educated. Of them, 4 daughters and three sons are married. All of them reside outside the village but all the unmarried children stay with him at the village.

More or less Das leads a happy life. But he faces some problems. His first problem is social and the second one is related to drawal of monthly pension from government treasury.

He says that 3 of his sons are employed, but do not contribute any money for the management of home. His first and third sons are doing business in Bhubaneswar and they are all settled there. His second son is a bank officer. He is in Allahabad... His eldest son is a miser, who stays in Bhubaneswar which is only 3 kilometers away from the village but he does not come to the village and he is not at all concerned about the health and well-being of his parents. Even, he does not contribute much towards the marriage ceremonies of his sisters or brothers. As the eldest son, he has some social, and economic obligations towards parents. But since he neglects his duties, other brothers also follow him and as a result parents become helpless to do anything... His second son, who is a bank officer in Allahabad, acts as if he is always busy. However, he does not get long-leave to come to the village. He rarely comes to the village. The nature of his 3rd son is more or less like that of the eldest son but somehow, he gives some money and looks after old parents. However he never demands money from him. He has two daughters and two sons still to marry. That is why he is disappointed. Whenever he becomes sick, he goes to his married daughters, who gladly provide medical care to him. He is treated well in the residence of his daughters.

As mentioned earlier, his second problem relates to the drawal of monthly pension from the treasury located in Bhubaneswar city. At this old age it becomes very difficult for him to come over to Bhubaneswar personally and draw the pension.

**Cast Study: 6**

Brahmananda Patra is a pension holder. His age is 62 years but he looks as if he is about 80-years-old. This is because of a number of social factors which he narrates with sorrow and agony.

He resides in the village Garhsrirampur. He has his wife, two sons and two daughters. His first son and first daughter are married. The rest two children are unmarried.

Amulya, eldest son of Brahmanda is a wayward person and not courteous. He got married to Charubala against the wishes of his family members. This was a love marriage.

Brahmananda was serving as a liberty attendant in Orissa University of Agriculture and Technology (OUAT). But he took voluntary retirement five years before the retirement age with a view to rehabilitating Amulya who is an under-metric. Amulya is now employed in OUAT as a tractor helper (Class IV) and gets around Rs. 2700/- (as per the opinion of Brahmananda) per month as his monthly salary.

Brahmananda says that, he left the job in order to employ his son with a hope that he would look after the parents. But he is totally indifferent. After Amulya was employed and handled ready cash, be became a drunkard and now behaving like a vagabond. Neither he cares for the parents nor for other relatives. Now he wants to sell all the landed property, but when his father protests he creates havoc in the family. One day Brahmananda proposed that the whole property be divided into six shares and, if he (Amulya) wants to sell, he may sell his own share but not the whole property. At this, he became furious and shouted at his father. Presently he is pressing his father to transfer the record of right to him. His father has told him that so long he is alive, it would not happen. But Amulya threatens his father that he would file a case against him and grab the whole property. In the last week when" he demanded to have the *patta*[1] and I did not give the key to open the trunk in which I had kept it, he rushed towards me with a position to give a slap and told that he would damage my limbs unless I give the *patta* to him. I resisted his behaviour and kept me mum in order to materialise the situation. But he has been telling me once and again that I have become an accubrance on him and so leave the house and go elsewhere... His wife follows him and behaves accordingly.

---

1 Documents relating to the record of right on landed property.

She is a selfish lady. I earn money but I am not given proper food according to my wish or requirement. She partialates in serving food. Whenever I fall ill my wife takes care of me but, my daughter-in-law hesitates to do any favour".

At the end of the discussion when the investigator put him a question regarding as to whom he (Brahmananda) loves most amongst his family members, surprisingly he named Amulya even when there were many persons in his family. The investigator did not understand. But he clarified that since Amulya is his eldest son, he has been psychologically attached to him from the very beginning of Amulya's birth. He wants that God should bless him so that he would become a gentleman.

**Case Study: 7**

Kunjalata is a family-pension holder. She is about 85-years-old. She resides in the village Satyabhamapur under Balianta block. She is *Karan* (scribe) by caste. Her husband was serving as a constable under Government of Orissa. Now, Kunjalata gets Rs. 1150/- per month as family pension.

Kunjalata has two daughters and two sons. All of them are married. Her eldest son Prabhat is a matriculate and is a marginal farmer. Her second son Prasant is a graduate. He is employed as a medicine representative. The family of both these children are staying together at village with Kunjalata. Prabhat has one son and one daughter. Similarly Prasanta has also one son and one daughter. Thus, altogether, Kunjalata has four grandchildren.

Most of the times Kunjalata spends her time with her grandchildren. She loves them very much. She is also quite happy with both her sons. But she is very displeased with her daughters-in-law since, she claims that they do not behave her property and do not lead life as per her wish or the demand of the society. However, when the investigator was interviewing Kunjalata he observed some uncustomary behaviour of her daughter-in-law which were not at all appreciating. Both of her daughters-in-law did not let Kunjalata free to talk with him alone. Either they appeared infront of him or watchdogged behind the wall in order to compel Kunjalata to deliver controlled-answers which must not go against any of them. On his several personal requests, there was also no result. Kunjalata was an intelligent old woman. She tried to answer many of the sensitive questions indirectly through various satirical remarks. However, from such remarks or answers, it was very clear for a lay man to understand the problems she was facing.

In order to give an impression of having a healthy social system, she pointed out various social behavioural practices of individuals which are diminishing in the present day society. According to her, these have disintegrated the interpersonal relationship among family members, particularly between parents-in-law and daughters-in-law to a great extend. She gives much tress on various ritual practices of Hindu life which she was performing earlier, i.e., when she was a young housewife. As per her opinion, (i) a daughter-in-law is the *Laxmi* (goddess of wealth and fortune) of the house. So, she must be very polite, soft-spoken and submissive; (ii) She must be very self-conscious about her dress. She should put veil when she is in front of her in-laws; (iii) She must obey and give due respect to her parents-in-law; (iv) She must observe the day-to-day festive occasions and rituals as per their own traditional rites. Otherwise there would not be happiness and prosperity in life.

Kunjalata said attitude, norms and values are changing very fast. People of her generation used to pay utmost respect to their elders, which has diminished with the younger generation at the present. At present some daughters-in-law not only pay scant respect to their parents-in-law but even torture and harass. This sort of attitude is pernicious and disruptive. When she was narrating her plight to the investigator her eldest daughter-in-law, who was listening their conversation at a short distance, rushed towards them like an injured lioness and brushed upon her. She demanded a very clear-cut answer from Kunjalata whether she meant her by what she had told the investigator. Kunjalata reacted very casually without giving any importance to the anger of her daughter-in-law. But the situation became very tensed and some aspects of the investigation remained incomplete. The investigator left the place without any further discussion with Kunjalata. Next morning when he reacted the house of Kunjalata she asked him, "did not you understand my problems yesterday" I have already told you all my miseries. What more questions you have to ask me now?" However, the investigator wanted to know from her as to who take cares of her when she falls ill. His question was very broad in nature and not specific for her daughter-in-law. But Kunjalata ironically said. "They (daughters-in-law) are all very good persons. Their food is not digested unless they take care of me... yesterday, after you left my home they have minded me not to tell anything against them. Now, tell me my son, when they do not permit me to talk to you and when they come forward, like adult men, to interact with the public, how do you expect that they would be taking care of me? Now I am 85-years-old. I wash my own clothes, and I always try to do my own work. However, when my sons are present they become showy and act as if they respect me and do some of my work, like washing my clothes and helping me to take bath at the village pond. But even if they help me in these day-to-day activities during the presence of my sons, they do it out of compulsion. I have very rightly observed how do they react silently. They are very intelligent. Hence their hesitation to do my work is not easily understood by my sons... However, my grandchildren are very loving. They love me heartily and I also love them alike".

Thus from the above discussion held with Kunjalata and the observation made at her house, it becomes very clean that there is a big gap in the social-bond between the daughters-in-law and parents-in-law, particularly with mothers-in-law. This is primarily because of the following facts:

*(i)* that there is a big generation gap between the parents-in-law and daughters-in-law;

*(ii)* the age-old traditional behavioural practices are not acceptable to the daughters-in-law. This, of course irritates the parents-in-law who are tradition bound;

*(iii)* that neither the daughters-in-law nor the parents-in-law love each other as their close kins. This might be due to the lack of blood ties between them;

*(iv)* that the attraction between grandparents and grandchildren is stronger than the attraction or social tie between parents-in-law and daughters-in-law; and

*(v)* that the grandparents get much pleasure or forget their miseries because of their grandchildren. They are a source of joy for the grandparents.

**Case Study: 8**

Chintamani Das is a pensioner. He was working as a constable under the Government of Orissa. He is now 71-years-old. He resides in the village Satyabhamapur of Balianta block. He is *Karan* (scribe) by caste.

Chintamani has three sons and three daughters. All of them are highly educated and are married. His first son is M.A. LLB. Second son is graduate. Third son is M.Com. They all work in Bhubaneswar and are also staying there even if their village is very close to this city.

Chintamani owns a very big paternal house at his village which has nine rooms. But none of his sons is residing at the village with him. Both, Chintamani and his wife face a lot of problems as regards the management of their paternal property with regard to agricultural land, kitchen garden, mango orchard, coconut groves etc. Apart from all these, their problems are also widely related to their health condition. Still then Chintamani and his wife do not stay with any of their sons. Chintamani says that "all my sons are very good in nature. They compel me and my wife to stay with them but I do not prefer since I do not get any freedom there. In the village there are about 10-12 retired persons. We have our *Thakur ghar* (village temple) where we all spend time either in playing cards or simply chit-chatting with one another or organise rituals like *Trinath-Mela* (worshipping of Brahma, the creator; Bishnu, the preserver and the Maheswar, the destroyer)... Moreover, I have my own house here which must be looked after; otherwise, venomous snakes will reside there... In Bhubaneswar, I do not get my friends and persons of my own status. Mostly, I have to spend my time within the four walls of the house. I feel very suffocated over there. However, I go to them whenever I feel to see my children and grandchildren but hardly I stay for a day or two with them". He is very much attached to the village where he had been brought up. The pleasant memories of his childhood lays in the village lark in his mind.

**Case Study: 9**

Sadasiva Mohanty is a man of about 70 years. His wife Sailabala is about 63 years. They belong to the village Bhainchua that comes under Balianta block. They are *Karan* (scribe) by caste.

Sadasiva has three sons and three daughters. All of them are college educated. All his sons are employed. His eldest son is serving in Bhubaneswar and also resides there. Rest two sons are working in the district of Mayurbhanj. Sadasiva and his wife are staying at their village. His only daughter who is unmarried is also staying with them and helps them in day-to-day life.

The social problems of Sadasiva are almost similar to that of Chintamani (Case Study: 8). However, he says that neither he nor Chintamani is dependent on their respective children. Their sons do not visit them regularly. In the first week of every month Chintamani goes to Bhubaneswar to draw his pension. But occasionally he visits the residence of his sons at Bhubaneswar. Now he is able to take care of himself. Time will show what will happen him when he falls sick. But he does not want to be a liability on his sons. Still he is hopeful that his sons would assume responsibilities of properties in the village. But they do not bother for it now and advise him to sell the whole property and stay with them in Bhubaneswar.

But Chintamani would not allow his property to be sold during his lifetime. He has deep attachment with his ancestral agricultural land and house. It is an emotional question for him.

**Case Study: 10**

Birendra Kumar Das is 69-years-old. He is working as a senior progress recorder under the State Government. Now he gets Rs. 1249/- per month as his position.

He resides in the village Bhainchua. His wife is alive. Her age is about 60 years. They have two sons and two daughters.

All of them are married except their second son. Both of their sons are unemployed and reside in village.

After retirement, Birendra lived with all his family members at the village. But after some years he took to *Mahima Dharma* and lived separately and lived separately from his family. He has built-up a small hut called' *Ashram'* at a short distance, i.e., about 200 meters away from his paternal house. At his paternal house his wife and other family members side together. He does not explain the reasons of his separation for the sake of maintaining a disciplined life as per the ideology of his *dharma*. However, in a nut-shell, he pointed out three broad reasons which indicate that his authority in his family was not recognised by his family members, particularly by his elder son. That is why he has been living separately in a hut. His wife is staying in the ancestral house alongwith his son and their families.

Even though he has left his home and is leading an *ashram*-life, he is not free from his family affairs. He donates three-fourths of his monthly pension to his family. In spite of this, his elder son does not show sympathy and due respect.

**Case Study: 11**

Pabitra Kumari (64) is the wife of A.C. Mohanty, a pensioner. Her husband was working as a clerk in the Department of Revenue, Government of Orissa.

She has four daughters and three sons. They are all married. All her sons are graduates and are employed. They stay in Bhubaneswar city.

Pabitra Kumari's husband is bedridden. He suffers from many diseases like falariasis, hypertension, asthma, and heart problem. Pabitra Kumari is also a patient but she is not bedridden. She suffers from obesity. Still then both of them stay together in the village and all their children are away.

Now Mohanty suffers from diarrhoea. He defecates on the inner verandah of his house and at times in his bed also. Pabitra Kumari takes care of her ailing husband. She says that though they have given birth to seven children, now, nobody is staying with them. All of the sons and daughters-in-law are staying at the places of their jobs, i.e., in Bhubaneswar. Mohanty loves very much his village and does not like to stay with any one of his sons in Bhubaneswar. Whenever he goes to Bhubaneswar, hardly he stays for a week or so with his sons and then comes back to the village. Now he is very serious and suffers from diarrhoea. Normally he stays with his youngest son at Bhubaneswar. But he does not stay there for long. Often he comes back to his village alone by hiring a rickshaw without informing his son. This is partly because of the ill-treatment of the wive of his son and partly because of his emotional attachment with his village. There is another factor which influences his mind to return to the village is that his wife becomes lonely in the village whenever he is away.

At this old age his wife is compelled to attend to all household work. She has to clean all the clothes of her husband and the floor. She does not have anybody to assist her. Therefore, she is leading a very wretched life with her ailing husband. Their sons are totally callous towards their ailing old parents. Both father and mother are in a pitiable condition.

Nowadays Mohanty has become very irritating and always demands nursing by his wife, who is not quite fine; she is also old and sick. Mohanty does not bother for her. He is a reprobate and very self-centred. He is most often rough and cruel in behaviour.

**Case Study: 12**

Bhaba Behera is a pensioner. He was working as a mohrir in the Department of Revenue, Government of Orissa. He is 65-years-old and his wife Suryamani is about 58 years. He is *Gauda* (milkman) by caste. His only source of income is his pension, which is merely Rs. 1472/- per month and there are five dependants on him.

Bhaba has one son and two daughters. His son and eldest daughter are married. His son is unemployed. Bhaba does not have any social problem but he is very much depressed as his son is unemployed. He says that his son is a very good person. He is very polite, well-behaved and disciplined. His wife is also alike He thanks God for giving him a nice son and a good daughter-in-law. Still he is very much depressed because his son is unemployed and the whole family depends on his paltry pension he gets. He apprehends that the condition of his family would be very miserable after his death. He gives many examples from his own village in which cases the children do not treat their old parents in proper manner but god has blessed them with good jobs. So it is his ill-luck that he has a golden son and a daughter-in-law, who are not in any salaried job. He attributes this distress condition to his past deeds.

**Case Study: 13**

Natabar Das is a man of about 70 years. He is a widower. He was working as a notice-server in the Income Tax Department, Government of India. Now he gets Rs. 1382/- per month as pension. He stays in the village Bhainchua where only one room is available.

He has two sons and four daughters. All are married except his 2nd son. His eldest son is employed who stays in Bhubaneswar. His second son is unemployed and stays with him in village.

Natabar is a poor man and he does not have much property which is sufficient even for these two persons to lead life comfortably. The eldest son of Natabar does not help them in any manner. He does not come to the village also. This creates constant psychological pressure in the mind of Natabar.

**Case Study: 14**

Biswanath Sahoo is a man of 63 years of age. He was working as a section officer in the Department of Public Health, Government of Orissa. He has retired from his service in 1993 and now gets Rs. 3700/- per month as his pension. He resides in his village Balianta (Talagarh). He has three sons and two daughters. All of them are married except his youngest son. They are all staying together.

Biswanath does not have any social problem which is related to his old age and family members. But he is depressed because of his retirement from his active life. He does not have any contemporary with whom he can spend his time. He finds himself very lonely and this loneliness creates some physical problem like rheumatism and depression. However as per the demand of the situation he plays cards with those whom he does not like much. Most often he goes to the river sites, sits alone and enjoys the beauty of the nature. This gives him much pleasure.

He points out some important problems regarding drawal of monthly pension. These are as follows:

*(i)* He draws pension from Treasury—II which is located at Bapujee Nagar, Bhubaneswar. For this he has to go by bus which is a strenuous work.

*(ii)* He has to wait there for a long time in queue.

*(iii)* There is no sitting arrangement inside the premises of the treasury. As a result, he has to stand continuously for a long time in the open air.

*(iv)* In some cases he has to go twice for drawing his pension.

*(v)* The treasury personnel fix up different dates for drawal of arrears. This creates an unnecessary and futile journey to Bhubaneswar.

**Case Study: 15**

Natabar Behera is a pensioner. He was working as a Khalasi under the Irrigation Department of Government of Orissa. Now he gets Rs. 1046/- as his pension. He is about 69 years. His wife is approximately 60 years or so.

Natabar has three sons. All of them are married and separated from one another. But they reside in the same compound. These, three sons practice milk business and are very much money oriented. Natabar gets Rs. 1046/- every month but none of his sons is interested to look after him and his wife since the cost of maintenance of two persons becomes more than what Natabar earns as his pension. However, presently they stay with their youngest son. But they are not satisfied with the food they are being provided. Nataber and his wife claim that the nature of each of their sons is good but their wives have made them self-centred, narrow-minded and stingy. More particularly the behaviour of the wife of their second son is very rough. The investigator was an eyewitness of improper behaviour when he was collecting data on his daily food. By the way of is discussion with Natabar, he told him that he and his wife do not get milk at bed time to which they were habituated when Natabar was earning. But his second daughter-in-law who was listening to their discussion without their knowledge at a distance and was not concerned in any manner with the discussion, immediately rushed to the spot and shouted in a violent mood that when their children do not get sufficient milk to drink, from where they would arrange it for the old people. In the mean time, purusotam (eldest son's son) interfered in the matter and supported his grandparents. And very rightly remarked that if his grandfather was not earning any money, by this time he would be sleeping alone at the *Polanga tota* (grove of caster trees or the graviyard) located at the near river basin. By this he meant that his grandfather might have died.

**Case Study: 16**

Kishor Chandra Das is aged 78 years. He is a retired government servant and draws Rs. 1016/- as his pension per month. He resides in the village Satyabahampur and is *Karan (Scribe)* by caste. He is a widower.

He has two sons and three daughters. All of them are married. His eldest so is a government servant who stays in Bhubaneswar with his family. His youngest son is working as a temporary worker in Irrigation Department of Government of Orissa. He and his family members reside in the village with his father.

Kisor says that, his sons are very good in nature and the nature and behaviour of his elder daughter-in-law is marvelous. She is very cultured, well-behaved and polite in nature. Whenever he visits them, she takes utmost care of him. She never takes food before serving them same to him. She is just like a *Devi* (goddess) and thus, she has no comparison. But my youngest daughter-in-law is very uncultured and adamant in nature.

Neither she respects him nor does any of his personal work, like washing of clothes or massaging of his body when he is sick. Whenever, he visits his elder son he stays with him for a fortnight or so. His village atmosphere attracts him most and as a result he comes back to his village. He says that although he is the real household head, he does not take any decision independently, since he has become old. Further, he says that he loves non-vegetarian food but he never gets it in his village.

# Index